The Orchid Mind

Cultivating the Ideal Conditions for Your Nature

Sandra Zecevic-Gonzalez

Counselling Psychologist & Accredited CBT Therapist

Founder, Orquidia Therapy

First published 2026

Published by Orquidia Press, London

Copyright © 2026 Sandra Zecevic-Gonzalez

Sandra Zecevic-Gonzalez has asserted her right under the Copyright, Designs and Patents Act 1988 to be identified as the author of this work.

All rights reserved. No part of this publication may be reproduced, stored in a retrieval system, or transmitted, in any form or by any means, electronic, mechanical, photocopying, recording or otherwise, without the prior permission of the publisher.

A note on case material: all client vignettes in this book — including the figures of Rita, Mark and Brenda — are composite characters drawn from many years of clinical practice. No individual client is represented. Any resemblance to specific persons, living or dead, is entirely coincidental. Identifying details have been changed throughout.

This book is intended as a general guide to psychological wellbeing and is not a substitute for professional clinical advice. Readers experiencing significant mental health difficulties are encouraged to seek support from a qualified health professional.

ISBN: 978-1-0676121-3-9

Typeset in Georgia

www.orquidiatherapy.com

For my father —

A creative orchid in every sense of the word.
And for all the orchids still learning to bloom.

Acknowledgements

This book has been a collaborative endeavour in every sense. I am grateful to the many clients, colleagues and supervisors whose insights, stories and wisdom have shaped my clinical thinking over more than twenty years of practice. The composite figures of Rita, Mark and Brenda carry fragments of many real experiences; I hope those who recognise themselves in them also recognise the deep respect with which they are held.

I am grateful to the researchers and clinicians whose work underpins every chapter — particularly W. Thomas Boyce and Bruce Ellis, whose *Orchid/Dandelion hypothesis* gave me a language for something I had long observed but not yet named; Paul Gilbert, Kristin Neff and Aaron Beck, who built the evidence base for the therapeutic approaches threaded throughout.

I am also grateful to friends who have supported and joined me in my creative adventures, which have been many. My parents and extended family members, all of you creative in your own way, several of you formally trained.

And lastly, to Danilo and Sebastian for personifying the soul of this book — resilient creatives who keep me grounded and nourish my roots.

A note on the creation of this manuscript:

The structure, content, frameworks, questionnaires and clinical tools in this book were conceived, directed and authored by Sandra Zecevic-Gonzalez. The manuscript was developed with the assistance of Claude, an AI system created by Anthropic, which supported the organisation, drafting and formatting of the text. All clinical judgements, theoretical positions and personal perspectives are entirely the author's own.

Table of Contents

How to Use This Book

This is not a book to be read passively. It is designed to be worked with at your own pace, in whatever order serves you best. Each chapter builds on the last, but each can also stand alone.

The book moves in two distinct phases. Parts One and Two build the foundations: the science of sensitivity, the conditions framework, and the evidence for why creativity is not a luxury but a clinical tool. There are reflection prompts and a self-assessment along the way, but these chapters are primarily about understanding. From Part Three onwards, the book becomes a working toolkit — CBT thought work, compassion practices, mindfulness, values clarification, sleep and body tools, creative rituals — that you can begin applying immediately. *If you are in acute distress, the guide below will direct you to the most relevant tools without needing to read in order.*

Nothing in these pages requires a therapist to unlock it. But if you are working with one, this book and the therapeutic relationship can be genuinely complementary. The book sets out the same integrative framework the author uses in her clinical practice, and works just as well alongside psychotherapeutic work as it does independently.

The reflection prompts and questionnaires are not optional extras. They are where the real work happens. Keep a dedicated journal alongside this book. Writing is itself a creative and therapeutic practice, and your words on those pages are data about yourself that no theory can provide.

Throughout these pages you will meet three people — Rita, Mark and Brenda. They are composites drawn from years of clinical practice, not case studies, but moments in which the concepts come alive in recognisable human experience.

If you are in significant distress, the final chapter will help you consider whether therapy might be the right next step. This book is a companion, not a replacement for that.

If you are struggling right now

1. **Go to Chapter 7 first:** If you are in significant distress, start at the end. Chapter 7 will help you assess whether you need professional support and what kind might be most appropriate.
2. **For anxiety and worry:** Begin with Chapter 4 (the Worry Period Technique and Thinking Errors table), then Chapter 1 to understand your sensitivity profile.
3. **For burnout and emptiness:** Start with Chapter 2 (Inner and Outer Conditions), then the Values Clarification section in Chapter 4.
4. **For disconnection and isolation:** Begin with Chapter 5 (Relationships and Creative Community), then the Conclusion (the 5-a-Day of Wellbeing).
5. **For sleep difficulties:** The CBT for Insomnia table in Chapter 4 offers immediate practical guidance.

Thriving is not a destination. It is a practice — and this book is your beginning.

Introduction

There is a story we tell about sensitive people. That they are fragile. That they feel things too much. That the world was not built for them and the best they can do is toughen up and learn to cope with it.

This book tells a different story.

The Orchid Hypothesis, one of the most significant findings in developmental psychology of the past thirty years, suggests that human beings exist on a spectrum of environmental sensitivity. At one end are the dandelions: robust, adaptable, capable of growing in almost any conditions. At the other end are the orchids: naturally responsive to their environment, vulnerable when conditions are wrong, but capable of extraordinary flourishing when conditions are right.

What the research confirms, and what twenty years of clinical practice have shown me, is that this is not a fixed identity. It is a state. Most of us move along this spectrum across our lives, often within a single year, a single relationship, a single job. Grief can turn a dandelion into an orchid overnight. The right creative community, the right work, the right quality of rest can move an orchid gently back toward centre. The question is never 'which one are you?' The question is always: 'what are your conditions right now – and what do they need?'

This book is built around three connected ideas.

The first is that your sensitivity – however it currently manifests – is not a flaw to be corrected. It is information. It is telling you something precise about the gap between the conditions you have and the conditions you need.

The second is that those conditions are cultivable. Not all of them, and not immediately — but more of them than you think, and more quickly than you might expect. The inner conditions: your thoughts, your nervous system, your relationship with your own emotions. The outer conditions: your work, your relationships, your physical environment, the broader environmental conditions you are living, your daily rhythms. This book gives you practical, evidence-based tools drawn from Cognitive Behavioural Therapy, Compassion-Focused Therapy, mindfulness, gratitude practice and a values identification tool, often used in Acceptance and Commitment Therapy.

The third idea is the one that surprised even me, after all these years of sitting across my clients in the therapy room. Creativity is one of the most powerful tools available for cultivating those conditions. Not creativity as performance. Not the pressure to produce something good or original or worthy of anyone's attention. Creativity as process — even for five minutes, even badly, even alone. The act of making, expressing, moving or imagining activates the parasympathetic nervous system, reduces cortisol and builds the *Soothing System* that chronic stress depletes. It creates a direct channel to the parts of yourself that anxiety and overwhelm tend to bury. A growing body of research — including a landmark 2019 WHO systematic review of over 900 studies — points clearly in the same direction. The clinical evidence is compelling. And the practice is available to every single person reading this, regardless of whether they have ever thought of themselves as creative.

The Orchid Hypothesis tells you what kind of plant you might be right now. The conditions work tells you what you need. Creativity is how you cultivate it.

This framework did not begin as a book. It began as a practice through the slow accumulation of what actually works, tested across years of clinical work with real people navigating real conditions: the young executive who could not stop overworking, the artist who had stopped painting, the parent who had given so much to everyone else that they had forgotten what they themselves needed.

Over time, a shape began to emerge from that work. Not a single theory but an integration: the Orchid Hypothesis as a framework for understanding vulnerability without pathologising it; CBT for the thinking patterns that keep people stuck; compassion-focused work for the self-criticism that underlies so much of what brings people to therapy; creativity as the practice that quietly holds all of it together.

What I found — and what this book attempts to offer — is that when these approaches are woven together, they do something none of them does quite as well alone: they give people a way to understand themselves that is both honest about difficulty and genuinely hopeful about change. This is at the heart of my integrative psychotherapeutic approach.

This is not a framework for getting fixed because there is nothing wrong with you. It is a framework for learning to tend to yourself, to the people you love, to the conditions that allow all of you to flourish. That tending is not a phase you complete. It is a practice you return to, season after season, with increasing skill and decreasing self-judgement. The orchid does not bloom once. It blooms when its conditions are right, rests when they are not, and with the right care, blooms again.

You do not need to be a permanent orchid to use this book. You need only to recognise that the conditions you are living in are not quite right for who you are and to want to change that.

That is enough. Let's begin.

PART ONE

Chapter 1: The Sensitivity Spectrum – Where Are You?

Before we can cultivate our optimal conditions for emotional wellbeing, we need to understand what kind of plant we are. Not in a fixed or deterministic sense. We, human beings, are far too complex for that. But in the sense of honest self-knowledge. What do we genuinely need in order to flourish? What environments nourish us, and what conditions deplete us?

The Orchid Hypothesis, originally proposed by developmental paediatrician W. Thomas Boyce and psychologist Bruce Ellis, offers a compelling framework for understanding this distinction.

Two Flowers, One Spectrum

The hypothesis draws on two plants as metaphors for the spectrum of human sensitivity. The dandelion grows almost anywhere – through pavement cracks, in neglected corners, in soils that would defeat more delicate organisms. Dandelion people are similarly resilient, tending to cope across a wide range of conditions without requiring specific conditions.

The orchid is entirely different. It requires specific conditions: indirect light, consistent moisture, protection from extremes. Place it in the wrong environment and it withers quickly. But place it in precisely the right conditions and it produces blooms of rare beauty and complexity that the dandelion, for all its resilience, could never produce.

Orchid people are equally responsive to their environment. They are often more sensitive to emotional atmosphere, to interpersonal tension, to noise and disorder, to criticism. They may be more prone to anxiety or overwhelm. But under the right conditions — supportive relationships, creative outlets, work that embraces their depth — they often demonstrate remarkable capacities for empathy, insight and meaning-making.

The orchid's sensitivity is not a flaw. It is the same quality that, in the right conditions, allows it to bloom more brilliantly than anything else in the garden.

A State, Not a Sentence

Boyce is emphatic: orchid and dandelion are not two boxes. They are the opposite ends of a continuous spectrum, and we may inhabit different positions at different times in our lives. A person who has functioned with dandelion-like robustness for years may, following bereavement or sustained overwork, find themselves suddenly orchid-sensitive. Equally, an orchid who invests consistently in understanding their optimal conditions may develop remarkable resilience — not the dandelion's robustness, but the orchid's particular strength born of deep roots and sustained nourishment.

Why Dandelions Become Orchids: The Role of Demands and Resources

Understanding why a person's position on the spectrum shifts requires us to look at the relationship between two things: the demands being placed on a person's system, and the resources available to meet them. When demands and resources are roughly in balance, when the pressures of life feel manageable and when we have adequate rest, relational support, and a sense of agency, most of us function closer to the dandelion end of the spectrum. We cope. We adapt. We recover.

But when demands begin to outstrip resources — through sustained overwork, bereavement, chronic relational conflict, or the slow erosion of sleep and self-care — something shifts. The nervous system, no longer adequately buffered, becomes more reactive. Minor stressors register more intensely. The emotional atmosphere of a room, the tone of a colleague's message, a small criticism that would once have washed over us: these begin to land differently. The threshold at which we are affected by our environment lowers.

Cognitive Behavioural Therapy would describe part of this process in terms of our beliefs about our ability to cope — what psychologists call self-efficacy. When repeated stress erodes our confidence that we can manage what life is asking of us, it does not merely affect our mood; it changes how we perceive and process incoming information. We become, in the precise sense of the Orchid Hypothesis, more susceptible to environmental influence. The dandelion has not become a different plant. Its conditions have changed, and with them, its sensitivity.

This matters both clinically and practically. It means that when you notice yourself becoming more orchid-sensitive — more easily overwhelmed, more reactive to your environment, less able to recover quickly — the most useful question to ask is not *what is wrong with me*? but *what has changed in my conditions*, and *what does my system need to recover its equilibrium*? Those are precisely the questions this book is designed to help you answer.

Orchid Sensitivity and Neurodivergence

Readers familiar with autism spectrum conditions, ADHD, or other forms of neurodivergence may notice points of overlap with the orchid profile: sensitivity to sensory input, a need for predictability and controlled environments, depth of processing, and heightened responses to social and emotional stimuli. This overlap is real, and worth acknowledging honestly.

Orchid sensitivity and neurodivergence are, however, distinct phenomena. Autism and ADHD are neurodevelopmental differences — differences in how the brain is wired, present from birth, and formally diagnosed through a structured clinical assessment process. They are not on a continuum with typical sensitivity; they represent a qualitatively different neurological profile. The orchid/dandelion framework, by contrast, describes a dimension of environmental sensitivity that appears to vary across the whole population, is influenced by experience and context, and shifts over time. It does not require and should not be used as a substitute for clinical diagnosis.

A NOTE

If you have an existing diagnosis of autism or ADHD, or suspect you may be neurodivergent, this book remains relevant to you: the tools for managing inner and outer conditions, building self-compassion, and cultivating a sustainable creative practice are directly applicable. But they sit alongside — not instead of — appropriate specialist assessment and support. If questions about neurodivergence are live for you, your GP or a clinical psychologist can help you access the right diagnostic pathway.

The Science of Sensitivity

One strand of research into sensitivity points toward a biological dimension. Studies of the NR3C1 gene — part of the glucocorticoid receptor system governing the body's response to cortisol — suggest that some people may carry a genetic predisposition toward heightened environmental responsiveness. Children carrying a variant of this gene who grow up in adverse conditions are significantly more likely to develop psychological difficulties.

But those same children, when provided with nurturing environments, do no worse than their less sensitive peers. In some studies, they have even been found to do better. The gene that creates vulnerability also creates receptivity.

But genetics is one pathway among several. Sustained stress, early relational experience, trauma, and the slow erosion of personal resources can all move a person toward orchid-sensitivity regardless of their genetic profile, as the previous section makes clear. The biological research is not a fixed verdict about who you are. It is simply further evidence that sensitivity is not a character flaw. It is information about your system — information that, understood properly, becomes a capacity to be cultivated.

This is the essence of what developmental psychologist Jay Belsky's important refinement of the original orchid/dandelion model calls the Differential Susceptibility Hypothesis. Where earlier frameworks emphasised sensitivity as a risk factor in adverse environments, Belsky's research demonstrates that sensitive individuals are more affected by their environments in both directions: more harmed by poor conditions, but also more enhanced by good ones. The sensitive person who finds their right conditions does not simply catch up with their less sensitive peers. In many domains, they surpass them. The sensitivity or receptivity to the environment, it turns out, is the advantage.

Michael Pluess's subsequent work on vantage sensitivity extended this finding in an important direction: highly sensitive individuals do not merely suffer more acutely when conditions are wrong, they benefit more substantially when conditions are right. Sensitivity, in other words, is an amplifier in both directions.

A NOTE

On the research landscape: *the Highly Sensitive Person framework by Elaine Aron, while clinically useful and widely applied, remains an area of scientific debate. Some researchers prefer to understand sensitivity as a continuously distributed trait rather than a distinct personality type. This book takes the position that both framings are complementary rather than competing: sensitivity exists on a spectrum (as Boyce, Ellis, Belsky and Pluess's work confirms). Aron's clinical descriptions of how high sensitivity manifests in daily life remain among the most practically useful in the field. Where the science is still developing, this book will say so.*

Where Are You on the Spectrum Right Now?

Before continuing, take a moment to locate yourself on the spectrum as it is right now, not as you imagine yourself in general, or at your best, or in calmer times. Today. This week. In your current conditions. The questionnaire below is not a diagnostic tool and it is not a personality test. It is a snapshot. A higher score does not mean you are permanently orchid-sensitive; a lower score does not mean you are immune to overwhelm. It means this is where you are right now, and that is exactly the information this book needs you to have.

Where am I on the Orchid-Dandelion Spectrum?

Rate each statement from 1 (not at all like me) to 5 (very much like me).

1. *I tend to notice and be affected by the emotional atmosphere in a room, even when nothing has been said overtly.*
   1 2 3 4 5
2. *I process experiences deeply and find that I need time alone after socially or emotionally demanding situations.*
   1 2 3 4 5
3. *I am more sensitive to criticism or disapproval than most people I know appear to be.* 1 2 3 4 5
4. *I feel things very intensely — both positive and negative emotions tend to be vivid and immersive.*
   1 2 3 4 5
5. *My wellbeing is strongly affected by the quality of my close relationships.* 1 2 3 4 5
6. *I am particularly aware of subtleties in my environment — noise, light, texture, tone of voice.* 1 2 3 4 5
7. *I tend to be conscientious and have a rich, complex inner life.* 1 2 3 4 5
8. *I find that my performance and mood vary considerably depending on external circumstances.* 1 2 3 4 5
9. *I tend to cope reasonably well regardless of the emotional climate around me. (R)* 1 2 3 4 5
10. *I recover from setbacks relatively quickly and do not dwell on difficulties for long. (R)* 1 2 3 4 5
11. *I can function well even in chaotic, noisy or unpredictable environments. (R)* 1 2 3 4 5
12. *I am rarely unsettled by criticism and tend to brush off disapproval. (R)* 1 2 3 4 5

Scoring guide: *Add your scores for items 1–8. Then add your scores for the reversed items 9–12 and subtract that total from the first. This gives you your net sensitivity score. A net score of 20 or above suggests you are currently operating with significant orchid sensitivity. Your nervous system is highly responsive to your environment right now, and the conditions work in this book is particularly relevant to where you are. A score of 10–19 suggests moderate orchid sensitivity. You are affected by your conditions but retaining reasonable resilience. A score of below 10, or a negative score, suggests you are currently closer to the dandelion end of the spectrum — you may be reading this at a moment of relative stability, or you may simply have a more robust baseline. Neither is better. Both are useful information. Remember: this is a snapshot of today, not a verdict about who you are. Come back to this questionnaire in three months, after a period of stress, after a holiday, after beginning a creative practice. The movement itself is data.*

Whatever your score, use it as a starting point for curiosity rather than a verdict. Mark your approximate position on the visual scale below:

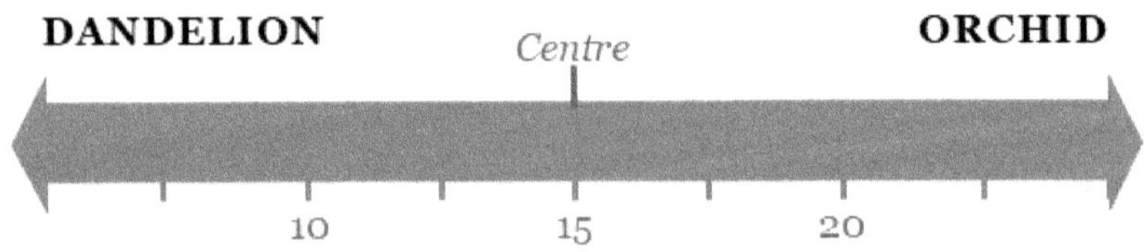

Throughout the book, revisit this assessment — your position on the spectrum may shift meaningfully as your conditions change.

Three Portraits: Rita, Mark and Brenda

Three individuals will accompany us throughout this book. They represent presentations I encounter frequently in clinical practice — not as diagnoses, but as human beings navigating particular challenges in particular conditions.

Rita, 35

Rita is a former ballet dancer who spent her late twenties in marketing, working in open-plan offices that never quite suited her — too loud, too exposed, too little space to think. She left to work independently three years ago, which helped. She is, however, currently feeling more anxious than usual and struggles to wind down. The constant tension triggers migraines, which GP visits confirmed are not due to a physical cause. She is currently exploring what her optimal conditions might look like to improve both emotional and physical health.

Mark, 27

Mark has always been the social, easy-going dandelion and the kind of person who moves through difficulty without being derailed by it. Last year, that changed overnight. His father died of cancer. His closest friend moved abroad. In the months that followed, panic attacks began. Then health anxiety. Mark barely recognises himself.

His story is a reminder that dandelions, too, can be overwhelmed — not because something is fundamentally wrong with them, but because some conditions exceed anyone's capacity to absorb.

Brenda, 42

Brenda has always been the strong one. Married with two young children, ageing parents nearby, a part-time job and the majority of household responsibilities. She has run on high-grade determination for years. Recently she has begun to weep unexpectedly and experience a terrifying blankness. Her conditions have been optimised entirely for others. Her own have been almost entirely neglected.

Orchids Who Changed the World

It is worth pausing, before we begin the practical work of this book, to name something that the history of human achievement suggests but rarely states plainly: many of the people who have contributed most profoundly to science, art, moral progress and our collective understanding of what it means to be human appear, by most available accounts, to have been orchids.

Charles Darwin spent years in painful solitude before finding the conditions in which his sensitivity to the natural world produced the most significant scientific theory of the modern era: a country house, a devoted family, a disciplined routine. He suffered chronic illness, avoided crowds, and needed long daily walks and quiet to think. In the right conditions, his capacity for patient, minute observation and his depth of feeling for living things produced work that changed everything.

Abraham Lincoln experienced what his generation called melancholy, a deep sensitivity to human suffering that would, in the wrong conditions, leave him prostrate with grief. He wept openly and often. He could not attend public executions. He felt the weight of others' pain as though it were physically present in his body. In the appropriate conditions — the terrible crucible of the Civil War, with his sensitivity fuelled by purpose, by language, and by a moral framework equal to the weight he carried – that same quality produced some of the most morally serious political leadership in recorded history.

Marie Curie, who described herself as acutely sensitive to atmosphere and interpersonal tension, found her conditions in the laboratory. In the patient, absorbed, detail-oriented focus that her sensitivity made natural, and her scientific genius made transformative. Jane Goodall's capacity to enter the world of chimpanzees as a neighbour rather than an observer, to notice what no observer had noticed before, was inseparable from the quality of sensitivity that others had spent her childhood trying to moderate.

Mahatma Gandhi's extraordinary capacity for moral clarity, for feeling the suffering of others as a call to action rather than a burden to manage, was the same quality that made him, in ordinary social contexts, exhausted by conflict and in need of extended silence and withdrawal.

Martin Luther King Jr., Princess Diana, Albert Einstein and Virginia Woolf are among other famous orchids that made enduring marks on human history, each transforming their field through the very sensitivity that others had spent their lives urging them to moderate.

None of these figures had it easy. Most suffered significantly – in the wrong conditions, at the wrong times, before they found what they needed. Darwin's illness. Lincoln's depressions. Woolf's breakdowns. Curie's isolation. What made the difference, in each case, was not the elimination of their sensitivity but the cultivation of conditions in which it became the very instrument of their contribution.

Orchid sensitivity has never been a barrier to greatness. It has, in the right conditions, been its source.

You are not being asked to become any of these people. You are being invited to take your own sensitivity as seriously as they eventually — sometimes painfully, often belatedly — learned to take theirs. The conditions they cultivated were particular to them. Yours will be particular to you. But the principle is the same: the sensitivity is not the problem. It is, in the right conditions, the advantage.

REFLECT

Where did your questionnaire score place you today? Does this feel accurate for your current conditions, or does it surprise you? Can you think of a time in your life when your score would have been significantly different? What were the conditions then? What changed?

✎ *Take a moment to write your response in a notebook before continuing.*

Chapter 2: Mapping Your Conditions – Inner and Outer

To thrive is not simply to feel better. It is to inhabit conditions within yourself and in the world around you that are genuinely suited to who you are. This chapter introduces the central organising framework of the book: the distinction between inner conditions and outer conditions, and the dynamic relationship between them.

Neither dimension is more important than the other, and neither can be fully addressed in isolation. A person who changes outer circumstances — moves cities, changes jobs, leaves a relationship — frequently discovers they have brought their inner conditions intact. The anxiety travels. The self-criticism follows. The relational patterns recreate themselves in new settings.

The Inner Environment

Your inner environment is the invisible ecology of your psychological life: the thoughts you habitually think, the beliefs you hold about yourself and the world, the emotional patterns that have become automatic, the ways your body carries stress, and the deeper values and meanings around which your sense of self is organised.

Core Beliefs

Core beliefs are deep convictions about ourselves, other people and the world formed primarily in early life through experience, relationship and sometimes trauma. They operate as filters through which all subsequent experience is interpreted. Common core beliefs that generate psychological difficulty include: 'I am not good enough', 'I am unlovable', 'The world is dangerous', 'I must always be in control' , 'I must be perfect or I am worthless'. These beliefs feel like facts. One of CBT's most significant contributions is the recognition that they are interpretations — and that interpretations can, with sustained effort, be revised.

Practising self-compassion and gratitude can help in reshaping harsh and rigid beliefs about oneself, others, and the world. Additionally, mindfulness plays a crucial role by allowing you to create distance from your thoughts, preventing you from automatically identifying with negative core beliefs that hinder personal growth. These will be elaborated on in Chapter 4.

Rita has carried the belief that she is too much for most of the rooms she walks into — too emotional, too intense, too easily affected by what others seem to take in their stride. Rita's core beliefs did not form through a single event but through a thousand small moments: the eye-roll of a friend, the ballet teacher who suggested she was being dramatic, the relationships in which she learned to adjust, quieten, diminish herself to be bearable. Core beliefs of this kind do not announce themselves as beliefs. Instead, they announce themselves as facts. The work of changing them begins with the recognition that they are not truths.

Thinking Patterns

Beneath core beliefs sit characteristic thinking patterns – the habitual cognitive shortcuts through which we make sense of daily experience. Under stress, these tend toward systematic distortion. The full catalogue of common thinking errors is also presented in Chapter 4, where we explore them as a practical tool for inner-condition work.

The Nervous System and the Body

The inner environment is not only psychological, but also profoundly physical. The state of the autonomic nervous system determines our baseline mood, cognitive functioning, capacity for creativity, and ability to connect with others. Chronic stress maintains the sympathetic (fight-or-flight) state, compromising the prefrontal cortex, sensitising the amygdala, disrupting sleep and digestion, and suppressing the immune system. The hormones adrenaline and cortisol prepare the body to respond to stressors, but chronic elevation can lead to negative health effects, including anxiety, weight gain, and other stress-related disorders. Understanding your nervous system's baseline is as important as understanding your beliefs.

Mark had always been the steady one. While his friends catastrophized, he coped; where others withdrew, he engaged. In the first few weeks following his father's death, he did not experience the acute grief reaction he had expected. Instead, he felt a kind of internal static, similar to a persistent low buzz of agitation that made it difficult to concentrate. His sleep became unreliable, and ordinary social events felt distressing in ways he had never encountered before. The move of his best friend abroad further isolated him, depriving him of someone who helped him feel secure and allowed him to talk things through. He did not recognise this as a nervous system in overload; rather, he interpreted it as a sign of weakness.

Understanding the distinction between an overwhelmed nervous system and a broken self that feels weak and defeated is one of the most important insights this chapter can provide.

Values and Meaning

A frequently overlooked dimension of the inner environment is the degree to which a person's life is aligned with their genuine values. When there is a significant gap between how we are living and what matters most to us, a persistent low-grade suffering tends to result, often without a clear identifiable cause. The Values Library in Chapter 4 provides a comprehensive resource for this exploration.

The Outer Environment

Your outer environment is everything outside the boundary of your skin that nonetheless shapes your psychological experience: your relationships, work, cultural context, physical surroundings, financial circumstances and the communities you belong to.

Relationships

Of all the elements of the outer environment, relationships consistently emerge as the most powerful determinant of emotional health. The quality of our attachments — to partners, friends, family, colleagues and community — predicts wellbeing outcomes more reliably than almost any other factor. If your nervous system is highly attuned, the quality of your closest relationships is often the single most decisive variable in overall psychological functioning.

Work and Purpose

Work occupies a central position in the outer environment. When it is meaningful, appropriately challenging and reasonably autonomous, it contributes significantly to wellbeing. When persistently demeaning, overwhelming or unsupported, it is one of the most reliable paths to burnout. The Work Conditions Questionnaire in Chapter 5 offers a structured framework for assessing your optimal professional environment.

Physical and Cultural Environment

Where we live, and the cultural context in which we live, shapes our inner world in ways that are easy to underestimate. Access to green space and natural environments reduces cortisol and restores attentional resources. Cultural messages — 'I must be productive to be worthy', 'Asking for help is weakness' — become internalised as personal beliefs over a lifetime. The relationship between the two columns on the following table run in both directions. Beliefs shape how we perceive relationships; relationships reinforce or challenge beliefs. Nervous system state affects how we experience work; the work environment affects the nervous system. Change anywhere in the system has the potential to generate change elsewhere.

Inner Environment	Outer Environment
Core beliefs about self and others	Intimate relationships and attachments
Habitual thinking patterns	Work, purpose and sense of contribution
Nervous system baseline state	Community, belonging, social connection
Emotional regulation capacity	Physical surroundings and access to nature
Body awareness and physical health	Financial and material security
Values alignment and sense of meaning	Cultural context and social norms
Self-compassion and inner voice	Creative and expressive opportunities

Brenda's situation illustrates how thoroughly these two dimensions can reinforce one another. Her belief that she must be strong — an inner condition formed early and held tightly — had led her to construct an outer life organised almost entirely around others' needs: a job managing everyone else's difficulties, relationships in which she was the reliable giver, a home from which her own creative practice had been quietly, progressively erased. Her inner conditions were producing her outer conditions. And her outer conditions were confirming her inner beliefs. In Brenda's life, as in most lives, understanding the cyclical relationship between her inner and outer conditions was the first step toward interrupting the cycle.

REFLECT

Identify two or three elements of your inner environment that feel most depleted or dysfunctional, and two or three elements of your outer environment that feel most nourishing or most toxic. Are there connections between them?

✎ *Take a moment to write your response in a notebook before continuing.*

PART TWO

Chapter 3: Why Creativity? The Science of Flourishing

Creativity, in the psychological sense, is not the production of great art. It is the capacity to generate something new from existing elements — to see connections, to experiment, to imagine alternatives, to express what is internal in forms that are external. This capacity is not rare. It is one of the most universal features of human mental life. And it is one of the most powerful tools available for cultivating optimal conditions in which emotional wellbeing can thrive. The science of creativity outlined in this chapter applies to everyone, but it may apply to orchids most of all.

Big C and Small c: Reclaiming Creativity for Everyone

Psychologists distinguish between 'Big C' creativity — epoch-defining breakthroughs — and 'small c' creativity: the ordinary, everyday acts of making, imagining, rearranging and expressing available to every human being. Planning a meal for friends, rearranging a room, finding an unexpected solution, writing in a journal, singing in the car — these are acts of creativity, and their psychological effects are real and measurable.

Rollo May's definition of creativity as 'bringing something new into being' is broad enough to include small, daily acts of engaged expressive living. Under this definition, every human being is capable of creative activity. The question is not whether you are creative, but whether you are creating and whether your life contains sufficient space and permission for it to occur.

Neuroplasticity and the Creative Brain

The brain is dynamic, adaptive and changeable throughout life, a property known as neuroplasticity. A simple illustration: when we learn a new route to work, the mental map we build becomes clearer and more automatic with repetition. When we practise mindfulness or creative expression regularly, the neural networks associated with those activities strengthen in the same way by building new pathways toward calm, perspective and flexibility.

The neuroscientist Michael Merzenich, whose research established many foundational principles of adult neuroplasticity, demonstrated that the brain continues to reorganise itself in response to experience throughout life, not just in childhood as was long assumed. What this means in practice is that the patterns of thought, emotions and nervous system activation that currently define your inner conditions are not fixed. They are the product of repeated experience, and they can be changed by new repeated experience. Creative practice, engaged in regularly and with genuine attention, acts as this kind of new repeated experience. Art therapy researcher Cathy Malchiodi's work on creative arts and neural integration further demonstrates that making, particularly image-making and movement, engages the brain's integrative processes in ways that purely verbal therapies may not reach.

Creative activity is one of the most powerful drivers of this process. Engaging in novel, generative, expressive activities promotes the growth of new neural connections and strengthens those associated with positive emotions, self-efficacy, cognitive flexibility and meaning-making. Regular creative practice literally reshapes the brain in the direction of greater resilience and adaptability which is the neurological equivalent of cultivating richer, more fertile soil.

Specific creative modalities have been associated with specific neurological benefits. Music activates multiple brain networks simultaneously — auditory, motor, emotional, memory — and has been shown to reduce anxiety, lower cortisol, improve mood and support recovery from neurological injury. Narrative and storytelling activate the brain's sense-making circuits, helping to organise and contextualise experience in ways that reduce its emotional charge.

One of the most striking recent studies in this area comes from Girija Kaimal and colleagues at Drexel University, who measured cortisol levels in participants before and after 45 minutes of art-making using a range of materials. The body's primary stress hormone, cortisol, reduced significantly in 75% of participants, regardless of their prior experience of art or their self-assessed artistic ability. Novices benefited as much as experienced practitioners. The act of making, not the quality of what was made, was the active ingredient. This single finding encapsulates much of what this book is asking you to trust: that the process matters more than the product. Beginning, even if imperfectly, without skill, and without an audience, is enough.

The World Health Organisation's 2019 systematic review of arts and health, which examined evidence from over 900 publications across 49 countries, concluded that engagement with the arts is associated with significant benefits across a wide range of physical and mental health outcomes, including reduced depression and anxiety, improved cognitive function, and enhanced social connection. The report's authors noted that the evidence base has strengthened considerably in recent years and that arts-based interventions are now considered a credible complement to clinical treatment rather than a peripheral nicety.

Creative Health: A Field Whose Time Has Come

The field of creative health has undergone a quiet revolution. In the UK, the National Centre for Creative Health's landmark 2023 Creative Health Review called for the integration of creativity into health and social care at every level. Arts Council England has incorporated creative health into its 2024–2027 delivery plan. Clinical trials through King's College London's SHAPER programme have demonstrated that creative interventions significantly improve quality of life across conditions including Parkinson's disease, postnatal depression and stroke. The WHO and the Royal College of Psychiatrists now both advocate for creative engagement as an essential component of public mental health strategy.

The most tangible expression of this shift is the *Arts on Prescription* model, in which GPs and social prescribing link workers refer patients to arts activities as part of their care. In 2023, social prescribing referrals in England surpassed NHS targets by 52%, benefiting over 1.1 million patients. A 2024 systematic review in Frontiers in Public Health, analysing thirty years of programmes, found consistent reductions in anxiety and depression. These effects accumulate with each referral cycle. What a GP can now prescribe for your mental health includes drawing, singing, writing and movement. The practice this book invites you into is the same one the health system is beginning, at last, to validate.

The creative health movement is not asking medicine to make room for the arts. It is demonstrating, study by study, that the arts were always medicine.

Creativity and the Three Emotional Systems

Paul Gilbert's Compassion-Focused Therapy framework describes three interacting emotional regulation systems. The *Threat System* detects danger, releases cortisol and adrenaline. It generates anxiety, anger or disgust and is frequently overactivated in modern life. The *Drive System* motivates pursuit of goals, energised by dopamine. The *Soothing System* promotes contentment, safety and connectedness, generating oxytocin and endorphins.

Creative activity is one of the most reliable pathways into the *Soothing System*. The state of absorbed, expressive, playful engagement that Mihaly Csikszentmihalyi called 'flow' quietens the *Threat System*, provides healthy occupation for the *Drive System*, and activates the *Soothing System*'s experience of presence and pleasure. For many people, this is the most direct route to a qualitatively different experience of being alive.

Self-Expression as Emotional Processing

Much of what causes psychological suffering is not simply the presence of painful feelings — it is their unprocessed, unexpressed accumulation inside us. Creative activity provides a structured medium for externalisation and processing. Writing transforms undeveloped inner experience into words: nameable, shareable, examinable. Visual art externalises what cannot be spoken. Music allows emotion to move through the body as well as the mind.

James Pennebaker's landmark research on expressive writing demonstrated that even brief periods of structured writing about emotionally significant experiences produced measurable improvements in immune functioning, reduced healthcare visits, improved mood and enhanced cognitive processing of difficult events. The benefit was not simply catharsis — it was the making of meaning.

Creativity is not an escape from your inner world. It is one of the most direct routes into it — and, with practice, through it.

Rita has always had a rich creative life — ballet classes, drawing, writing in journals, attending theatre. In her most difficult periods, these are precisely the activities she abandons first, dismissing them as self-indulgent. Working together, we identified this pattern: under stress, her *Threat System* pushes her into anxious productivity and her *Soothing System* becomes starved. This in turn causes tension and potentially contributes to migraines. Reintroducing a small daily creative practice that was non-negotiable and unattached to any standard was one of the most significant interventions in her therapy, which helped her *Soothing System* to recharge and reduce stress and tension.

Mark used to express himself through sport and music. He played guitar informally with friends. Since his bereavement, he has abandoned both. In sessions Mark explored how those activities were, without his realising it, his primary access routes to the *Soothing System*. The suggestion of returning to ten minutes a day with the guitar — no audience, no expectation, just playing — was initially resisted strongly. 'I'm not in the mood.' That, his therapist said, is precisely why it matters now.

The Orchid State and Creativity

There is one further dimension worth naming explicitly. The neuroscience of creativity outlined in this chapter applies to everyone, but it may apply to orchids most of all. If you are currently feeling highly sensitive, if you process experience more deeply and respond more strongly to environmental stimuli, you are likely carrying a nervous system that is more easily dysregulated by chronic stress and more readily restored by experiences of safety, meaning and flow. Creative engagement addresses all three of those needs simultaneously: it down-regulates the *Threat System* through absorption and present-moment focus; it activates the *Soothing System* through self-expression and the quiet satisfaction of making; and it engages the *Drive System* in a form that is self-directed, intrinsically motivated and free from the evaluative pressure that so often makes high-sensitivity a liability in conventional work and social settings. This is why creativity is not simply a useful addition to the orchid's toolkit. For many orchids, it is the condition that makes all the other conditions possible.

REFLECT

When did you last engage in a genuinely creative activity without it needing to produce anything for anyone else? What stopped you doing it more often? What would change in your inner conditions if you protected time for it regularly?

✎ *Take a moment to write your response in a notebook before continuing.*

PART THREE

Chapter 4: Cultivating Inner Conditions

The inner environment does not change through insight alone. Understanding why we think and feel as we do is valuable, but it is not sufficient. Change requires practice: the repeated, patient application of specific tools that, over time, build new cognitive, emotional and physiological habits. This chapter presents the most important inner-condition tools drawn from CBT, mindfulness, compassion-focused therapy and the science of values.

Working With Thoughts: The Landscape of Thinking Errors

One of CBT's most foundational contributions is the identification and classification of cognitive distortions: systematic ways in which anxious or depressed thinking diverges from accurate perception. The first step toward changing them is to recognise them.

A NOTE

An important distinction: unhelpful vs inaccurate thoughts: Not all negative thoughts are distortions. Sometimes things genuinely are difficult or have genuinely gone wrong. CBT is not an invitation to replace hard thoughts with relentlessly positive ones. That would be neither credible nor useful. The goal is balance: a thought that accounts for all the evidence, honestly acknowledges difficulty, and does not amplify suffering beyond what the situation justifies.

The table below provides a comprehensive list of thinking errors.

Thinking Error	**What it looks like**	**Rebalancing question to ask yourself**
All-or-Nothing Thinking	'If I'm not perfect, I'm a total failure.' No middle ground or shades of grey exist.	Is there a middle position here? What would a 70% outcome look like?
Catastro-phising	Automatically anticipating the worst possible outcome: 'If I make one mistake I'll be fired.'	What is the most likely outcome? What is the evidence for the worst case?
Mind-Reading	Assuming you know what others think — usually negatively: 'Everyone at that meeting thought I was incompetent.'	What evidence do I actually have? Could there be another explanation for their behaviour?
Fortune-Telling	Predicting negative outcomes as though they were facts: 'This relationship will fail just like the others.'	Am I predicting or knowing? What would need to be true for a different outcome to occur?
Emotional Reasoning	Treating feelings as facts: 'I feel stupid, therefore I am stupid. I feel worthless, therefore I am worthless.'	What are the actual facts of this situation, separate from how I feel about it?

Thinking Error	**What it looks like**	**Rebalancing question to ask yourself**
Should Statements	Rigid internal rules: 'I should always be calm. I must never need help. I ought to manage this alone.'	Who set this rule? Is it based on evidence or assumption? What would I say to a friend who said this?
Personali-sation	Taking disproportionate responsibility: 'My child is struggling — I must be a bad parent.'	How many factors other than my actions contributed to this outcome?
Filtering	Focusing exclusively on negatives while discounting positives:	What am I ignoring or discounting? What would the full picture include?
Labelling	Attaching a global negative label to oneself: 'I'm a loser.' 'I'm an anxious person.' 'I'm broken.'	Would I label a friend this way based on one event? What more accurate and specific description could I use?
Magnifica-tion & Minimisation	Magnifying your failures and minimising your successes — or the reverse with others.	Am I applying the same standard to myself and others? What would an objective observer say?
Jumping to Conclusions	Acting on assumptions without seeking evidence: assuming the worst before checking facts.	What is the most charitable alternative explanation? What would I need to find out?
Control Fallacies	Feeling either responsible for everything ('I must fix this') or helpless about everything ('There's nothing I can do').	What is actually within my control here? What is not — and can I practise releasing it?

No one commits all of these errors equally. Most people have a characteristic cluster — two or three patterns that appear reliably under stress. Identifying your own cluster is one of the most practically useful pieces of self-knowledge available.

To see how this works in practice, consider Mark in the weeks following his father's death, when his health anxiety was at its most acute.

Mark noticed a persistent stomach-ache one morning and within minutes had concluded that something was seriously wrong with him, that he was ill, that it would be cancer, that he would die as his father had, alone and too soon, before he had lived the life he had imagined for himself. By the time he arrived at his therapy session, he had spent three hours in a state of acute physiological fear.

Working through the thinking errors table together, several patterns became recognisable: **catastrophising** — the stomach-ache had become a terminal diagnosis in a matter of minutes, each thought escalating the last without any evidence to support the leap. **Emotional reasoning**: *I feel terrified, therefore something must genuinely be wrong*. **Mind reading**: *My GP will think I'm wasting her time if I call*. And beneath all of it, a quieter distortion that is common in grief: **personalisation** — a half-formed, unexamined belief that his father's illness meant something about his own body's fragility, as though vulnerability were inherited rather than circumstantial.

The balanced response did not require Mark to dismiss his fear or pretend the stomach-ache wasn't there. It required only that he examine the evidence, as he would for anyone else. *What do I actually know right now?* A stomach-ache, present for one morning, in a person who has been sleeping poorly and under sustained emotional stress for several months. *What are the most likely explanations?* Tension. Disrupted eating. Grief, carried in the body, which, for many people, settles precisely there. *What would I say to a close friend who told me this?* That he should eat something, rest if he could, and call his GP if it persisted beyond a few days, not because something was certainly wrong, but because that is the reasonable, proportionate response. That reframe did not eliminate Mark's anxiety. But it created enough distance between the feeling and the conclusion to interrupt the spiral. Over time, and with practice, that distance became easier to find and the spirals shorter.

The Thought Record: A Five-Step Practice

1. **Situation:** Briefly describe the event or moment that triggered the difficult feeling.
2. **Emotion:** Name the emotion(s) and rate their intensity (0–100%).
3. **Automatic thought:** What went through your mind? Write it exactly as it appeared.
4. **Thinking error:** Which distortion from the table above is present?
5. **Balanced response:** What would a fair, evidence-based, compassionate response be? Re-rate your emotion.

REFLECT

Review the thinking errors table. Which two or three patterns show up most reliably in your own inner life — especially under stress? Can you recall a recent situation where one of them was active? Write down the automatic thought and practise writing a balanced response.

✎ *Take a moment to write your response in a notebook before continuing.*

The Worry Period

Worry has a seductive internal logic. It feels like preparation, as though by turning a problem over repeatedly in the mind, we are doing something useful, staying one step ahead of whatever might go wrong. If your nervous system is finely attuned to threat, worry can feel not just useful but necessary: a form of vigilance that keeps danger at bay.

The difficulty is that worry is not problem-solving. It circles rather than advances. Genuine problem-solving moves toward a conclusion, a decision made, an action taken, a situation accepted as beyond our control. Worry returns, reliably, to the same starting point. It consumes the cognitive and emotional resources that actual problem-solving requires, whilst generating the neurological stress response as though the feared event were already happening. The body cannot distinguish between a real threat and a vividly imagined one. Every cycle of worry is, in that precise physiological sense, an experience of the thing we are most afraid of without any of the resolution that facing it directly might bring.

The Worry Period Technique

1. **Schedule**: Designate two 15-minute 'worry periods' each day — e.g. 8am and 6pm.
2. **Contain**: When worry arises outside these periods, note it briefly and postpone it: 'I will think about this at 6pm.'
3. **Use the time**: During the worry period, give the concern full attention. Problem-solve where possible; distinguish actionable concerns (I can do something) from hypothetical ones (I cannot control this).
4. **Close**: At the end of the period, consciously close it. Redirect attention to the present. Over time, the habit of continuous background worry weakens.

Values Clarification — Your Values Library

One of the most important questions for inner-condition work is this: are you living in a way that is genuinely aligned with what matters most to you? When our daily choices — how we spend our time, our energy, our attention — are persistently out of step with our deepest values, a low-grade suffering tends to result.

The following table provides a comprehensive Values Library to draw from. It is not exhaustive but it covers the most commonly significant domains.

Values Library		
Character & Integrity		
Authenticity	Loyalty	Trustworthiness
Courage	Reliability	Wisdom
Honesty	Responsibility	
Integrity	Self-discipline	
Relationships & Connection		
Belonging	Forgiveness	Nurturing
Compassion	Friendship	Partnership
Community	Generosity	Service
Empathy	Kindness	Support
Family	Love	
Growth & Learning		
Adaptability	Expertise	Learning
Challenge	Growth	Open-mindedness
Curiosity	Improvement	Perseverance
Education	Knowledge	Reflection
Creativity & Expression		
Aesthetics	Creativity	Music
Art	Expression	Poetry
Beauty	Imagination	Storytelling
Craft	Innovation	Vision
Achievement & Purpose		
Ambition	Impact	Meaning
Competence	Leadership	Purpose
Contribution	Legacy	Recognition
Excellence	Mastery	Success

Values Library		
Freedom & Autonomy		
Adventure	Individuality	Spontaneity
Autonomy	Privacy	Travel
Freedom	Self-direction	
Independence	Simplicity	
Wellbeing & Balance		
Balance	Mindfulness	Security
Health	Nature	Spirituality
Humour	Peace	Vitality
Joy	Play	Wellness
Leisure	Rest	
Justice & Society		
Diversity	Justice	Sustainability
Equality	Respect	Tolerance
Fairness	Social responsibility	

On Values and Permission

A common difficulty, particularly among people with Brenda's profile — the strong ones, the carers, the ones who always manage — is that they know perfectly well what their values are, but feel they have no right to act on them. 'That's for when the children are older.' 'I can't afford that luxury.' If this resonates, add a sixth question to the exercise: What has historically stopped me living this value? The answer often reveals a core belief that deserves attention in its own right.

Brenda grew up in a large family with limited resources, where there was always someone who needed more than she did. The lesson she took — never quite spoken, but absorbed completely — was that prioritising herself meant taking from others. And whenever she tried to make space for her own interests, a second belief surfaced quietly beneath the first: 'If I don't do it, who will?' Not a question, really. A reminder of how long she had been holding things together alone.

When Brenda completed the values clarification exercise, she was surprised by her results. She listed creativity, beauty, connection and play in her top five. None of which appeared anywhere in her current week. Her daily life was almost entirely organised around obligation (work and home responsibilities) and care for others. Beginning to reintroduce even small doses of her values such as an hour of pottery on a Sunday morning at a local art centre, was not indulgence. It was irrigation.

Values Clarification Exercise (ACT)

1. **From the Values Library above**, circle or note all the values that resonate with you — don't filter yet.
2. **From those**, identify your top ten, then narrow to your five most essential.
3. **For each of your top five values,** rate how well your current life reflects it (0 = not at all; 10 = fully).
4. **Where the gaps are largest**, ask: what one small action this week could bring my life slightly more into alignment with this value?

5. **What** has historically stopped me living this value? Write your honest answer.
6. **Return** to this exercise every three months. Values, and the gaps between them and our lives, shift over time.

Mindfulness: Building the Observing Self

Mindfulness is the practice of deliberately directing attention to present-moment experience — thoughts, bodily sensations, emotions — and observing what arises without trying to change or escape it. This quality of non-judgemental observation is not passive; it is a specific, trainable skill, and one of the most reliably effective tools available for interrupting the ruminative cycles that sustain anxiety and depression.

The evidence base is substantial. Mindfulness-Based Stress Reduction (MBSR), developed by Jon Kabat-Zinn, has been shown across multiple trials to reduce symptoms of anxiety, chronic pain and stress-related conditions. Mindfulness-Based Cognitive Therapy (MBCT), which integrates mindfulness with CBT techniques, is now a recommended treatment for recurrent depression in the UK's clinical guidelines. The mechanism is not mysterious: regular mindfulness practice strengthens the brain's capacity to observe thoughts without being captured by them, creating the small but crucial distance between a feeling and a response that makes change possible.

If your nervous system is finely tuned to environmental input, this distance is particularly valuable. Thoughts and emotions can feel totalising: not something you are having, but something you are. Mindfulness does not eliminate that intensity. It builds the observing self: the part of you that can notice the intensity without being entirely consumed by it.

A Five-Minute Foundational Mindfulness Practice

1. **Sit:** Find a comfortable, upright position. A soft downward gaze is fine; closed eyes are not required.
2. **Anchor**: Bring attention to the sensations of breathing – the rise and fall of the chest or belly.
3. **Notice**: When your attention wanders to thoughts, plans, worries, just notice that it has wandered. This noticing is the practice.
4. **Return**: Gently, without self-criticism, return attention to the breath. Repeat as many times as needed.
5. **Close:** After five minutes, expand awareness to the whole body and the sounds in the room. Notice how you feel, descriptively, not evaluatively.

Self-Compassion: The Most Radical Inner Condition Change

For many people who come to therapy – particularly those with orchid sensitivity, perfectionism or a rescuer pattern – the most resistant and most transformative area of work is the quality of the relationship they have with themselves. Kristin Neff identifies three components of self-compassion: mindfulness (seeing suffering clearly); common humanity (recognising that difficulty is part of shared human experience); and self-kindness (treating oneself with the warmth one would offer a good friend).

Rita had spent years trying to solve the problem of herself. The dancer who was not quite good enough had become the professional who worked harder than anyone else in the room, quietly filling the space that dance had left with other forms of usefulness. She had not recognised this as grief. In the self-compassion work, something shifted. Not through reframing or argument, but through the practice of turning toward the teenager who walked out of that audition room and never spoke about it — and meeting her, for the first time, with warmth rather than verdict. The loss had been real. The pain had been real. Rita had simply never given herself permission to say so. What she had needed, all along, was not to be less — but to stand beside herself with compassion.

There is a pervasive misconception worth naming directly: that self-compassion means lowering standards, or that it is a luxury reserved for those who have not worked hard enough for their suffering. The research says precisely the opposite. Self-criticism undermines performance, resilience and creative risk-taking. Self-compassion improves all three. It is not the opposite of excellence. It is, in fact, its condition.

If you are currently in a heightened sensitivity state, self-compassion may feel dangerous at first, as though letting go of self-criticism would mean losing all motivation or becoming complacent. This fear is understandable and worth sitting with, rather than dismissing. The practice below is a beginning.

The Self-Compassion Break (Neff)

1. **Acknowledge**: In a moment of difficulty, pause: 'This is a moment of suffering. This is difficult.'

2. **Humanise**: Remind yourself this connects you to others: 'Suffering is part of life. Many people feel this way.'

3. **Offer kindness**: Place a hand on your heart if it feels right. Ask: what would I say to a good friend feeling exactly this? Say that to yourself.

4. **Return**: Return to whatever you were doing, carrying the softer tone with you.

Gratitude Practice: Retraining Attentional Bias

The anxious mind has a well-documented negativity bias — a tendency to scan for threat, register difficulty, and discount what is going well. This is not a character flaw; it is an adaptive inheritance. But if your nervous system is already primed for environmental responsiveness, this can mean that the painful aspects of experience consistently crowd out the nourishing ones, even when both are present in equal measure.

Gratitude practice works by deliberately counteracting this bias. Emmons and McCullough's foundational research found that people who wrote regularly about what they were grateful for showed significantly higher wellbeing, more positive affect, and better sleep than control groups. Seligman's Three Good Things exercise — writing down three things that went well each day, and their causes — is one of the most replicated interventions in positive psychology, producing measurable reductions in depression sustained over months. Gratitude, by directing attention toward what is present and good rather than absent or threatening, activates the *Soothing System* in a way that is both immediate and, with practice, cumulative.

The mechanism matters. Gratitude does not require pretending difficulty does not exist; it requires holding difficulty and goodness simultaneously, which is a more accurate picture of most lives than the threat-focused version the anxious mind tends to produce. For orchid people who process the painful with great depth, developing an equal capacity to dwell in what is good is not a spiritual exercise but a neurological one: it builds new attentional pathways that create a more balanced inner landscape over time.

✎ *Try it for two weeks before deciding whether it suits you*

Three specific things, noted in writing at the end of each day: something you noticed, something that worked, something or someone you are glad exists. Specificity matters more than scale — the quality of light through the kitchen window counts as much as good health. Try it for two weeks before deciding whether it suits you.

The Body as Inner Condition: Nutrition, Sleep and Movement

Nutrition and the Gut-Brain Connection

Approximately 90% of the body's serotonin is produced in the gut. The health of the gut microbiome, directly influenced by diet, is therefore a determinant of mental health in a literal biological sense. The Standard American Diet, high in refined sugars and processed carbohydrates, creates chronic inflammation and blood sugar instability that contribute directly to mood swings, anxiety and fatigue. The principle is simple: prioritise real food over processed food, slow-acting carbohydrates over fast-acting ones, and adequate protein to support serotonin production.

The gut-brain connection is one of the most rapidly developing areas in neuropsychology. Research by John Cryan and Ted Dinan at University College Cork – who coined the term 'psychobiotics' for dietary interventions that act on mental health via the gut – has established that the microbiome communicates directly with the brain through the vagus nerve, influencing mood, stress reactivity and cognitive function. Their work suggests that dietary choices are not merely a matter of physical health but of psychological conditions in the most literal sense: what you eat shapes the inner environment in which your thoughts and emotions arise.

Sleep and CBT-I

Sleep is the inner condition's most fundamental maintenance system. During deep sleep, the hippocampus processes the emotional events of the day, filing memories and reducing their emotional charge. Chronic sleep deprivation disrupts this process, leaving the nervous system hyperreactive and the prefrontal cortex compromised.

CBT for Insomnia (CBT-I) is the recommended first-line treatment for chronic sleep difficulties – more effective in the long term than medication. The table below provides a practical overview of its core components.

CBT-I Technique	What it involves	Why it works	Practical notes
Sleep Restriction	Limit time in bed to actual sleep time only; build sleep pressure	Consolidates fragmented sleep; rebuilds the sleep-wake rhythm	Your therapist calculates your initial 'sleep window' (e.g. 11pm–6am); this widens weekly as efficiency improves
Stimulus Control	Bed used for sleep only; get up if awake >20 min	Breaks the habit of lying awake; re-associates bed with sleepiness	No reading, phones or worrying in bed. If awake, go to another room and return when sleepy
Sleep Hygiene	Consistent wake time; caffeine curfew; dark/cool room; limit screens 1hr before bed	Reinforces circadian rhythm; reduces physiological arousal	Same wake time every day — even weekends — is the single most important hygiene rule
Cognitive Restructuring	Identify and challenge anxious beliefs about sleep	Reduces the 'performance anxiety' around sleep that perpetuates insomnia	'I must get 8 hours' → 'My body will get what it needs if I provide the right conditions'
Relaxation Training	Progressive muscle relaxation, diaphragmatic breathing, mindfulness scan	Lowers physiological arousal; activates parasympathetic nervous system	Practise daily, not only at bedtime — relaxation is a skill built through repetition
Paradoxical Intention	Lie in bed with eyes open, intending to stay awake	Removes the effort and anxiety of 'trying to sleep', which is self-defeating	Counter-intuitive but effective: the pressure to sleep is often what prevents it

CBT-I typically takes six to eight sessions and produces durable results. The initial days of sleep restriction feel uncomfortable – building what sleep scientists call 'sleep pressure' – but the improvement in sleep quality that follows is substantial and lasting.

Exercise and Movement

Movement is one of the most direct and well-evidenced routes to improved inner conditions. Regular physical activity increases serotonin, dopamine and endorphins, reduces cortisol, improves sleep quality and sharpens concentration. These effects are not incidental to psychological wellbeing but central to it. A study published in JAMA Psychiatry found that exercise can be as effective as antidepressant medication for mild to moderate depression. This is worth sitting with: the body moving through space is, in measurable terms, medicine.

If you are highly sensitive, the nature of the movement matters as much as the fact of it. High-pressure, competitive or performance-oriented exercise can activate the *Threat System* rather than soothe it – producing more cortisol, not less, and activating the *Drive System*'s competitive achievement-orientated circuitry rather than the *Soothing System*'s restorative one. Movement that carries a meditative, creative or social dimension tends to serve the orchid nervous system more reliably: a walk in nature, yoga, dance, swimming, gardening. Research from the University of Exeter found that nature-based activity produced significantly greater improvements in mood and wellbeing than equivalent indoor exercise: a finding that will surprise no one who has ever noticed how differently they feel after twenty minutes outside versus twenty minutes on a treadmill.

The goal is not athletic performance. It is nervous system regulation. Choose movement that your body actually wants to do, in conditions that feel safe and undemanding, and do it consistently. That is enough.

Hormones, the Body and Orchid Sensitivity

One of the most important and most frequently overlooked inner-condition influences on orchid sensitivity is hormonal. Oestrogen plays a significant role in regulating serotonin receptor sensitivity and modulating the HPA axis, the body's primary stress-response system. This means that hormonal transitions do not simply affect mood in a general sense: they directly alter the threshold at which the nervous system responds to its environment. A person who has functioned with relative dandelion robustness for years may find, during a period of hormonal flux, that they have become measurably more orchid-sensitive, more affected by noise, conflict, emotional atmosphere, and the demands of daily life, without any corresponding change in external circumstances. This is not psychological weakness. It is physiology.

Two life stages illustrate this particularly clearly:

Adolescence brings a dramatic reorganisation of the hormonal system alongside significant neural remodelling of the prefrontal cortex, the brain region responsible for regulating emotion and moderating threat response. The combination creates a period of heightened environmental responsiveness that is entirely normal and developmentally appropriate, but which can feel, from the inside, like something has gone profoundly wrong. For young people who are constitutionally orchid-sensitive, adolescence can amplify that sensitivity to an intensity that is genuinely difficult to bear. Understanding this, that the nervous system is not broken but in a period of major construction, can be one of the most relieving reframes available, both for adolescents themselves and for the adults around them.

Perimenopause presents a parallel picture at the other end of the reproductive lifespan. As oestrogen levels decline and fluctuate during the perimenopausal transition (a process that can begin a decade before the final menstrual period and is rarely linear), many women notice a significant shift in their emotional and sensory experience. Sleep becomes more fragile. Anxiety that was previously manageable becomes intrusive. Emotional reactivity increases. Tolerance for noise, crowds, conflict and overwhelm decreases. For women who have always been orchid-sensitive, this can feel like a sudden loss of the coping capacity they had worked hard to build. For women who had previously identified more as dandelions, it can be profoundly disorienting, feeling a sense of not recognising themselves. In both cases, the explanation that is most helpful is also the most accurate: this is the nervous system responding to a change in its hormonal conditions. The tools in this book of inner and outer condition management, self-compassion, values-based living, creative practice are particularly well-suited to this transition, because they work *with* the nervous system rather than against it.

It is worth noting that hormonal sensitivity is not confined to oestrogen or to women. Testosterone fluctuations in adolescent males contribute to the same pattern of heightened environmental reactivity. The postpartum period involving a sharp drop in oestrogen and progesterone following birth creates another window of orchid-like vulnerability that affects parents of all genders through disrupted sleep, the demands of a newborn, and the profound identity shift of new parenthood. The premenstrual phase of the cycle, in which progesterone falls and serotonin availability dips, is a monthly reminder of how directly biochemistry shapes sensitivity. Wherever hormonal flux appears in a life, the appropriate question is the same: what conditions does my system need right now, in this particular phase, to feel adequately resourced? That question, and the habit of asking it without self-criticism, is itself a form of inner-condition work.

REFLECT

Looking at your current inner conditions, which area feels most in need of attention? Which of the tools in this chapter would you most like to experiment with this week? Make it specific: what will you do, when, and for how long?

✎ *Take a moment to write your response in a notebook before continuing.*

Chapter 5: Cultivating Outer Conditions

Having attended carefully to the inner landscape, we turn to the outer. For you, outer conditions can be the decisive factor in whether psychological growth or suffering prevails. This chapter explores the most significant dimensions of the outer environment and offers frameworks for assessing and cultivating each one .

Relationships: The Most Powerful Outer Condition

The quality of our attachment relationships is the single most consistent predictor of emotional wellbeing in the research literature. John Cacioppo's decades of research on loneliness demonstrated that chronic social disconnection is as physiologically damaging as smoking. Conversely, secure, reciprocal, trusting relationships buffer against almost every form of adversity.

What Cacioppo's research establishes is that connection matters. What the psychotherapist Carl Rogers identified, through decades of clinical observation and research, is that not all connection nourishes equally and that the *quality* of relational experience may matter as much as its presence .

Rogers proposed that the most emotionally healing relationships share three core conditions: *empathic understanding* (being genuinely heard and comprehended, not merely listened to); *unconditional positive regard* (being accepted without conditions attached to that acceptance); and *congruence* (an authenticity in the other person, a sense that they are genuinely present rather than performing a role). Originally proposed as the conditions required for therapeutic change, Rogers' framework has since been supported by research showing that these same qualities predict the healing power of relationships outside the consulting room — in friendships, partnerships and families. If your sensitivity is currently high, your capacity to detect inauthenticity, conditional acceptance and emotional absence tends to be finely tuned — and the presence or absence of these qualities is rarely subtle. The relationships that genuinely restore tend to be those in which all three conditions, at least in some measure, exist.

For many readers, the significance of this quality is seldom an intellectual exercise. Your nervous system may be finely attuned, picking up on subtle nuances—a dismissive tone here, a superficial warmth there, or the palpable shift in atmosphere when a friendship has shifted to become one-sided. This heightened awareness is not a manifestation of paranoia; rather, it reflects a profound accuracy in perception. The challenge lies in learning to trust this innate sensitivity, recognising it as valuable information rather than dismissing it as mere oversensitivity. By embracing this gift, you can navigate your relationships with greater clarity and authenticity, drawing upon your insights to foster deeper connections and nurture your wellbeing.

The following exercise begins with the relationships that already hold the qualities Rogers describes. Those are the ones worth tending first.

Mapping Your Relational Conditions

1. **The inner circle:** Who are the two or three people with whom you feel most genuinely yourself – seen, accepted and safe? Do you invest enough time in these relationships?
2. **The draining relationships:** Which relationships consistently leave you feeling worse than you started? Are there patterns – people who reliably activate your *Threat System*?
3. **The gap:** Is there something you need from your relational environment that is currently absent – genuine intimacy, reliable support, creative companionship?
4. **The reciprocity question:** In your closest relationships, is care flowing in both directions? Or are you primarily a giver – and if so, at what cost?

As Mark has withdrawn from his social world in the wake of his grief, his outer conditions have deteriorated in a way that reinforces his anxiety. Part of his recovery involves the gradual, gentle rebuilding of connections, not through forcing sociability he does not feel, but through identifying the one or two friendships in which he feels enough safety to begin to be honest about what has happened to him and how tender he feels about it.

Finding Your Optimal Work Conditions

Work – whether paid employment, caregiving, creative practice or study – occupies a central position in the outer environment. When it is meaningful, appropriately challenging, reasonably autonomous and sufficiently recognised, it contributes significantly to psychological wellbeing. When it consistently fails to provide these things, a pervasive sense of futility or resentment tends to develop.

Rita had spent several years working in a busy open-plan marketing agency, telling herself that the constant noise, rapid task-switching and relentless social demands were simply how work was: that everyone found it as draining as she did, and that her end-of-day exhaustion was the normal price of a career. It was not until she began freelancing and working from a quiet room with natural light, a clear boundary between working hours and rest, and the freedom to choose her collaborations, that she understood the difference between conditions she could survive and conditions in which she could flourish. The questionnaire below is designed to help you map that difference for yourself, before it takes a decade to discover it by accident.

The concept of person-environment fit captures something essential: it is not whether a job is objectively good or bad, but whether it is right for the particular person in it. Understanding your own requirements – not what you think they should be – is fundamental. The questionnaire below is designed to help you identify the specific work conditions in which you are most likely to flourish.

Optimal Work Conditions Questionnaire

Rate each statement from 1 (not at all like me) to 5 (very much like me).

1. *I do my best work in a quiet, low-stimulus environment with minimal interruptions.* 1 2 3 4 5
2. *I need natural light and an aesthetically pleasant, comfortable physical space to function well.* 1 2 3 4 5
3. *I am most productive working privately — from home or a dedicated space — rather than in open-plan settings.* 1 2 3 4 5
4. *I prefer a structured day with clear schedules and predictable routines over a flexible, self-directed one.* 1 2 3 4 5
5. *I work best when I can focus deeply on one thing for extended periods rather than switching frequently between tasks.* 1 2 3 4 5
6. *I am most energised by abstract thinking — ideas, theories, big-picture questions and complex concepts — rather than concrete, practical tasks.* 1 2 3 4 5
7. *I am drawn to creative and imaginative work: generating ideas, possibilities and original solutions.* 1 2 3 4 5
8. *I feel most engaged when my work involves making meaning or serving a larger purpose, not only producing measurable outputs.* 1 2 3 4 5
9. *I prefer to work independently most of the time, with the option to collaborate when I choose.* 1 2 3 4 5
10. *I find meetings and collaborative sessions energising and generative rather than draining.* 1 2 3 4 5
11. *I need clear supervision and regular feedback rather than being left entirely to self-direct.* 1 2 3 4 5
12. *I need clear boundaries between work and personal time. I struggle to restore when work bleeds into evenings and weekends.* 1 2 3 4 5

13. *I need unscheduled time in my week — space for rest, creative replenishment and spontaneity.* 1 2 3 4 5

14. *I would benefit significantly from flexible working arrangements that accommodate variable energy and emotional needs.* 1 2 3 4 5

15. *My work needs to be aligned with my core values otherwise I find it difficult to sustain motivation and wellbeing over time.* 1 2 3 4 5

Scoring guide: *Rather than producing a single total, this questionnaire maps your profile across five domains. Within each, a score of 4 or 5 on any item indicates a genuine need — not a preference, but a condition your working environment should, wherever possible, reflect.*

Items 1–3 *(physical environment): high scorers are significantly affected by noise, light and privacy. Open-plan or unpredictable spaces are likely to deplete you more than most.* ***Items 4–5*** *(structure and focus): high scorers need either predictability or sustained depth — frequent interruptions and task-switching are not merely annoying but genuinely costly to performance and wellbeing.* ***Items 6–8*** *(thinking style): high scorers are most engaged by meaning, abstraction and creative possibility. Work that is purely transactional or disconnected from a larger purpose tends to feel hollow quickly, regardless of other compensations.* ***Items 9 and 14*** *high,* ***items 10 and 11*** *low (autonomy): one of the most common profiles for readers of this book, and one of the most frequently in tension with conventional employment structures.* ***Items 12–14*** *(work-life integration): high scorers need the boundary between work and restoration as a psychological necessity, not a lifestyle preference. Without adequate recovery time, performance and emotional regulation both deteriorate.* ***Item 15*** *(values alignment): when work is persistently misaligned with what we most deeply care about, no amount of good management or pleasant colleagues fully compensates. Values misalignment is a slow depletion — rarely dramatic, but cumulative and serious.*

Once you have completed the questionnaire, write a brief Work Conditions Profile for yourself: a short description, in your own words, of the environment, thinking style, social arrangement and life-integration that your scores reflect. Where you can, distinguish between preferences (what you would like) and genuine needs (what you require to function well). This profile is not an idealised wish list; it is a map of your actual requirements. Use it in conversations with managers, when considering new roles, or simply as a more honest way of understanding your own history with work.

REFLECT

How closely does your current work environment match your Work Conditions Profile? Where are the most significant gaps? What is one realistic change — however small — you could make or advocate for in the next month?

✎ *Take a moment to write your response in a notebook before continuing.*

The Creative Community: Shared Expression as Outer Condition

One of the most powerful and undervalued outer-condition resources is the experience of shared creative expression. Research on group music-making, choir singing, collaborative art-making and community theatre consistently demonstrates benefits beyond those of individual creative practice: synchronisation of physiological states, the experience of belonging to something larger than oneself, reduction of social isolation, and the particular trust that develops between people who have made something together.

The Yale-Harvard study of choir participation found significant increases in life expectancy among members — likely reflecting the combination of creative, physical, social and purposeful dimensions that group singing uniquely combines. Research on the vagus nerve suggests that singing together specifically stimulates this nerve, promoting social bonding and emotional regulation at a physiological level.

The idea of a creative community may carry a particular anxiety alongside its appeal. The same sensitivity that makes creative expression so necessary also makes the vulnerability of sharing it feel considerable. This is worth acknowledging directly: the first time you sing in a group, show someone a piece of writing, or bring a handmade object into a room of others, something genuinely tender is involved. The research on group creative practice suggests, however, that this vulnerability is precisely what makes it so effective. The shared risk, the collective permission to be imperfect, the discovery that making something together generates a different quality of belonging than almost any other activity. These are not incidental to the experience. They are the experience.

Brenda, who had spent years 'having to be competent and strong' in every room she entered, found her first pottery class unexpectedly disquieting. Alongside the mild anxiety of taking off the mask of competence, she felt moved. Not because her work was good but because for once she was in a room where no one expected it to be. There was no pressure and she felt liberated.

For people whose outer conditions are depleted in the dimensions of community, creative expression and soothing-system activation, joining or creating a space for shared creative practice may be one of the most efficient outer-condition investments available.

Physical Environment and Access to Nature

Research in environmental psychology consistently demonstrates that access to natural environments – parks, water, trees, light – reduces cortisol, lowers blood pressure, restores depleted attentional resources and promotes the parasympathetic state. Even brief daily exposure to natural settings has measurable wellbeing effects. If your nervous system registers environmental inputs more intensely, you are likely to be particularly responsive to these factors and may benefit disproportionately from intentional attention to your physical surroundings.

Orchid people often know this intuitively and discount the knowing. They notice that they think more clearly by a window. That they recover more quickly after a walk in a park than after an hour on a sofa. That the quality of light in a room, the level of background noise, the aesthetic of a space affects their mood in ways that feel disproportionate – and so they learn to apologise for the noticing rather than embrace the experience. The sensitivity that registers these things is the same sensitivity that, in the right conditions, enables depth of perception, emotional intelligence, and creative attention. Treating your physical environment as a legitimate and serious outer-condition variable, not a luxury to be earned, not fussiness to be overcome, is one of the simplest and most consistently overlooked acts of self-care available to you.

When the Soil Itself Is Compromised

The conditions framework in this book operates on the assumption that change is possible — that with sufficient understanding, the right tools, and genuine commitment, the inner and outer environment can be cultivated toward flourishing. That assumption holds for most of the people likely to be reading these pages. But it would be dishonest, and clinically incomplete, not to acknowledge what it cannot account for: the conditions that exist beyond individual agency entirely.

Poverty is not a lifestyle variable. Chronic financial insecurity — the kind that makes basic safety feel provisional, that forecloses choice at every turn, that requires the entire nervous system to operate on permanent alert — is itself a condition of the soil. If your nervous system is already finely tuned to threat and instability, economic precarity does not merely add stress to an otherwise manageable life. It saturates the environment in a way that makes almost every other intervention harder to sustain. You cannot reliably practise self-compassion when you are frightened about the rent. You cannot protect creative time when you are working three jobs to survive. The research on poverty and psychological wellbeing is unambiguous: scarcity is not a character failing. It is an environmental condition with profound neurological consequences, and it deserves to be named as such.

The same is true of environments shaped by conflict, displacement or systemic violence. War, persecution and forced migration do not merely create acute trauma. They destroy the outer conditions at their most fundamental level: safety, continuity, belonging, the sense that the ground beneath one will hold. For anyone navigating any of these realities, the question is not how to optimise conditions but how to survive their absence. Therapy, in these circumstances, must begin with the ground itself, with safety, stabilisation and the slow rebuilding of what was taken, before any of the frameworks in this book can be meaningfully applied.

Closer to the everyday experience of many readers is the dysfunctional work environment: the organisation that systematically undermines autonomy, that rewards performance over wellbeing, that tolerates or perpetuates cultures of criticism, unpredictability or chronic overload. A persistently toxic work environment is not merely unpleasant. It is, in the most literal sense, a condition that corrupts the soil. The five-a-day practices, the values work, the creative rituals — all of these can offer genuine relief, but none of them can fully compensate for an environment that is actively working against the nervous system every day. In these situations, the most important clinical question is not how to cope better but whether the environment is one that can be changed, negotiated with, or, where neither is possible, left.

This is not a counsel of despair. People demonstrate extraordinary resilience in conditions that should, by every measure, prevent it. Creativity survives poverty; connection survives displacement; dignity survives dysfunction. But it would be a quiet form of cruelty to present a framework for flourishing without acknowledging that some conditions lie outside the individual's power to cultivate. When that is the case, the failure belongs to the conditions, not to the person living within them.

REFLECT

Looking across the dimensions of your outer environment — relationships, work, community, physical surroundings, and the broader conditions in which you are living — which feels most nourishing? Which most depleted? What is one small, specific change you could make in the next week to improve one area where change is genuinely within your reach?

✎ *Take a moment to write your response in a notebook before continuing.*

Chapter 6: Creative Rituals – Building a Sustainable Practice

Knowledge of the benefits of creative practice changes nothing. What cultivates the conditions for emotional wellbeing is practice: regular, repeated creative engagement that is protected from time pressure, self-criticism, perfectionism and the demands of others that so reliably erode it.

Recovering Your Creative History

Before building a new creative practice, it is worth looking back. Most people who say 'I am not creative' were creative as children. But someone or something, at some point, persuaded them otherwise. A teacher's comment. A performance that did not go as hoped. The arrival of adult responsibilities that made play feel like a dispensable luxury. The voice that says: there is no point if I am not good at it.

For many people, the hardest part of building a creative practice is not finding the time or the technique. It is the quiet, unexamined belief that they forfeited the right to one somewhere along the way. Rita did not stop dancing because she lost interest or because life became too busy. She stopped because a panel of judges in one room on one afternoon told her, in effect, that she was not good enough to do it professionally, and she heard something that was never actually said: that she was not good enough to do it at all. These are not the same thing. The standard required to dance in a professional company and the standard required to dance are not in conversation with each other. One is about excellence in a competitive field. The other is about what your nervous system needs, what your body remembers, what your inner life requires to stay oxygenated. Rita lost both when she only needed to lose one. What this chapter asks you to consider, before we look at the enemies of creative practice and how to dismantle them, is whether something similar happened to you, and whether the verdict you have been carrying was ever really yours to keep.

REFLECT

What is your earliest memory of doing something creative — making, imagining or expressing something, simply for the pleasure of it? When did you stop doing that thing — or something like it? What interrupted it? If you could recover one creative activity from your past with no pressure to be good at it, what would it be?

✎ *Take a moment to write your response in a notebook before continuing.*

The answers to the above questions often reveal both the path back and the obstacles that block your creativity. The two most common obstacles — perfectionism and the tyranny of productivity — deserve to be named directly before we begin.

The Enemies of Creative Practice

Perfectionism insists that anything worth doing, must be done well – which means, in practice, that anything that cannot be done to a high standard had better not be started. Creative activity, by its nature, requires tolerance for the imperfect, the exploratory, the uncertain and the unfinished.

The tyranny of productivity treats creative time as a luxury to be earned. 'I don't have time for that' is rarely a factual statement – it is a values statement, revealing that the activity has been placed below other priorities. For people whose inner conditions include deep-seated beliefs about needing to justify their existence through usefulness, this is particularly powerful and particularly worth examining.

Five Principles for a Sustainable Creative Practice

Principles for a Sustainable Creative Practice

1. **Small and regular over large and occasional**: Twenty minutes of drawing every morning is more sustaining than a full day in a studio twice a year. Benefits accumulate through consistency.
2. **Process over product:** The goal is not to produce anything but to inhabit a particular quality of engaged exploratory attention. Release attachment to the output.
3. **Non-negotiable and protected**: Treat your creative time as you would a medical appointment. It is not the first thing to be sacrificed when life becomes demanding. It is, at those moments, the most important thing to preserve.

4. **Permission to be terrible:** The inner critic's standards are not welcome in the creative space. The only standard that matters is engagement: are you here, paying attention, making something?
5. **Variety and experimentation**: A creative practice evolves. Try different modalities — writing, drawing, music, movement, cooking, gardening — and notice which ones you return to.

A Menu of Creative Modalities

Expressive Writing

Writing is the most accessible creative modality: it requires no equipment, no training, no talent. Expressive writing about emotionally significant experience, without concern for style or audience, has a substantial evidence base. Pennebaker's research protocol involves writing continuously for 15–20 minutes on three to four consecutive days about a topic that has been emotionally significant, exploring both the facts and the feelings. The benefit derives from making meaning: taking fragmentary inner experience and translating it into coherent narrative form.

✎ ***Try this week: Writing***

Choose a topic you have been turning over — something unresolved, unexpressed, or simply persistent. Set a timer for 20 minutes. Write without stopping, without editing, without re-reading. When it is finished, close the notebook. You do not need to share it with anyone.

Notice what has shifted, if anything. It may take several days for you to identify it.

Visual Art and Making

Drawing, painting, collage, ceramics, textile work — any activity that involves making something with hands and materials — engages the body as well as the mind, activating sensory processing that can quieten the verbal, ruminative circuits of anxious thinking. You do not need to be able to draw. Doodling, colouring, tearing images from magazines and arranging them: these are sufficient. The quality of engagement matters more than the quality of the result.

The physiological evidence is striking. Girija Kaimal's research at Drexel University measured cortisol levels before and after 45 minutes of art-making and found significant reductions in 75% of participants regardless of their prior experience with art. The novices benefited as much as the experienced. It was the act of making, not the skill of the maker, that produced the effect. This single finding is worth holding on to whenever the inner critic insists you are not creative enough to begin: the biology does not care about your technique.

Art therapy researcher Cathy Malchiodi, whose work integrates neuroscience with creative arts practice, describes visual art-making as a form of neural integration, a way of processing experience that bypasses the verbal, analytical circuits of the prefrontal cortex and engages sensory, emotional and somatic networks simultaneously. For people whose difficulties are held in the body rather than accessible through words — a common profile in trauma, anxiety and burnout — this makes visual art-making not just a pleasant activity but a clinically meaningful one.

✎ ***Try this week: Visual Art***

Buy an inexpensive sketchbook and a set of coloured pencils or markers. Set aside 15 minutes. Make marks — any marks. You do not need to represent anything. The goal is hand moving, eyes on paper, mind engaged with something that has no consequences.

Notice what happens. You don't need to record it.

Music and Singing

Of all the creative modalities, music may have the most extensively documented effects on the brain and body. Neuroscientist Stefan Koelsch's research has demonstrated that music activates a broader network of brain regions simultaneously than almost any other human activity — engaging auditory, motor, emotional, memory and social processing circuits in parallel. This is not incidental: it means that musical engagement, even simply listening with full attention, constitutes a form of whole-brain activation that few other activities can match. Playing or singing adds motor and proprioceptive dimensions that deepen the effect further.

Singing, especially in groups, activates the vagus nerve, synchronises physiological states between participants, reduces cortisol and promotes the soothing-system state. Daisy Fancourt's research at University College London, which tracked 258 people in choral groups over a year, found measurable improvements in mental health, immune function, sense of social bonding and quality of life, effects that accumulated over time and were particularly pronounced in people who had been experiencing depression or anxiety at the start of the study. You do not need to sing well. You need only be willing to open your mouth and make a sound.

Beyond everyday practice, music therapy has established a substantial clinical evidence base. It is used in stroke rehabilitation to reactivate speech and motor function through the brain's musical memory circuits, which often survive neurological injury even when language circuits do not. It is used in dementia care to reach people whose verbal memory has been severely compromised but whose emotional and musical memory remains intact. It is used in PTSD treatment to regulate the nervous system when verbal processing of traumatic material is not yet possible. Music is not merely pleasant. In the right circumstances, it is medicine.

✎ ***Try this week: Music***

Choose three songs you love and sing them privately — in the shower, in the car, in the kitchen. Notice what happens in your body when you do. The resistance you may feel is worth observing: it often marks exactly the place where the *Soothing System* most needs access.

No performance. No audience. Just you and the sound.

Movement and Dance

Movement-based creativity addresses the dimension of emotional experience most directly held in the body — which is, for many people, exactly where it needs to be addressed. Bessel van der Kolk, whose clinical and research work on trauma has reshaped how the field understands the relationship between body and mind, argues that the body is not simply a vehicle for the brain but a primary site of emotional experience and storage. Traumatic and chronic stress experiences are encoded in the nervous system, in muscular tension, in patterns of breath and movement. They cannot be fully resolved through verbal or cognitive work alone. Movement, van der Kolk's research suggests, reaches what talking cannot.

Research by Lewis and Lovatt demonstrates that improvisational, unstructured movement promotes divergent thinking — the capacity to generate multiple perspectives and solutions — while structured dance activates convergent thinking, the focused mental processes required to find a specific answer to a problem. Both forms have value, and the distinction is a useful one: when you need creative expansiveness, move freely; when you need focused problem-solving, move with structure.

Peter Lovatt's research on dance and cognitive function has produced one of the most striking findings in the field: improvised dance improves cognitive flexibility in people with Parkinson's disease, a condition characterised by rigidity in both movement and thought. The implications extend well beyond clinical populations. If improvised movement can create new neural pathways in a brain affected by Parkinson's, the same principles apply to the neural rigidity that anxiety, depression, burnout and chronic stress produce in all of us. Dance — particularly unstructured, self-directed, private dance — is not an indulgence. It is a form of neural rehabilitation available to anyone.

✎ *Try this week: Movement*

Put on three minutes of music you love and move without choreography in your kitchen or in your bedroom with the door closed if needed. There is no correct way to do this. Simply follow what your body wants to do. If resistance arises — embarrassment, self-consciousness, a voice that says this is ridiculous — notice it and move anyway. The resistance and the medicine are often the same thing.

Notice what remains when the music stops.

Everyday Creativity

Creativity does not require a dedicated practice or a specific modality. It can be cultivated in the texture of everyday life: cooking a new dish with genuine attention, rearranging a space, approaching a problem from an unexpected angle, telling a story to a child, photographing what caught your eye on a morning walk. The quality of attention — curious, playful, exploratory, generative — is what makes an activity creative, not its form.

The psychiatrist and play researcher Stuart Brown, whose decades of research traced the role of play in healthy development across the lifespan, found that play-deprived adults, those who had systematically removed exploratory, non-purposive activity from their lives, showed higher rates of depression, rigidity and interpersonal difficulty. Play, in Brown's framework, is not the opposite of work: it is the condition that makes meaningful work possible. What this book calls everyday creativity is, in Brown's terms, the adult form of the play that keeps the self alive and responsive.

You now have both the science and the practice. You understand what kind of plant you might be right now, and what conditions you need. You have the tools to begin cultivating them — inner and outer — and the creative practices to sustain that work over time. What remains is to put it together into a daily shape that is genuinely yours. That is the work of the final pages.

REFLECT

Which creative modality most calls to you? Design a small creative ritual for the next two weeks — specific in its form, its timing and its duration. Write it here as a commitment to yourself.

✎ *Take a moment to write your response in a notebook before continuing.*

The Conditions: Putting It Together

This book has offered you three things. First, a way of seeing yourself that makes honest sense of your experience — that explains, without pathologising, why you are more affected by your conditions than others appear to be, and why this sensitivity is not a flaw but a form of responsiveness that can be cultivated into genuine advantage. Second, a set of evidence-based tools for understanding and shifting both the inner conditions (thoughts, nervous system, emotional patterns, values) and the outer ones: work, relationships, community, physical environment. Third, and most importantly, a practice: the daily, patient, non-judgemental act of creative engagement as the primary mechanism through which all of those conditions can be nourished and sustained.

None of this is quick. None of it is linear. There will be weeks when the conditions feel almost right and weeks when they feel impossibly far away. The research on lasting psychological change is unambiguous on one point: the mechanism is not vivid insight; it is consistency, however modest. The accumulation of small daily choices, made in the direction of your own flourishing, is what cultivates the conditions over time. Not perfectly. Not heroically. Just repeatedly.

To help make that consistency possible, the following framework draws together the book's essential threads into a single structure you can return to every day.

The 5-a-Day of Wellbeing

Adapted from the New Economics Foundation's Five Ways to Wellbeing and enriched by the Orchid Hypothesis and the creativity research threaded throughout this book, The 5-a-Day of Wellbeing offer the simplest possible answer to the question: what shall I do today? Each condition can be met in minutes. Their power lies not in any single day but in the cumulative effect of their combination over time.

Two adaptations have been made to the original framework: Keep Learning has been reframed as Creating. Give, oriented outward toward others in the NEF framework, has been reframed as Restoring, oriented inward toward the self. For an audience characterised by high sensitivity, creative disconnection and chronic over-giving, these are not cosmetic changes. They reflect the specific clinical argument of this book.

Noticing

The cultivation of present-moment awareness: the practice of actually being in your own life, rather than perpetually running slightly ahead of it into plans and worries. Without the capacity to notice — your thoughts, bodily sensations, emotional state, the quality of the moment you are actually in — no other condition can be cultivated with any depth. Noticing can be practised in any moment: the texture of sunlight on a wall, the taste of the first sip of coffee, the quality of your breathing right now.

Moving

The body needs to move, not as an obligation or a performance metric, but as a basic requirement of physical and psychological health. Daily movement reduces cortisol, increases serotonin and endorphins, and shifts the nervous system away from the sympathetic activation of stress. Where possible, choose movement that nourishes other conditions simultaneously: a walk in nature (noticing); dancing to music you love (creating); exercise with a friend (connecting).

Connecting

Daily, intentional investment in even one genuine connection — a conversation that goes beyond the transactional, a moment of real contact, an act of generosity toward someone in your community — has measurable wellbeing effects. The quality of attention matters more than the duration. When we most want to withdraw, connection is most important: the nervous system co-regulates with others, and isolation removes the most powerful calming resource available.

Creating

Daily engagement with some form of creative expression (however small, private or imperfect) maintains the neural pathways of generativity, sustains the *Soothing System*, and keeps the inner environment oxygenated. Each day: make, express or imagine something. A sentence in a notebook, a doodle in a margin, a photograph, a meal given genuine creative attention, a problem approached from an unexpected angle. This is the condition around which this book has been built — because it is the one that most directly and reliably cultivates all the others.

Restoring

The most frequently neglected and, for many people, the most radical condition: deliberate, daily restoration. Not the passive collapse of scrolling or background television, but real rest: sleep, stillness, activities that activate the *Soothing System* without demanding anything in return. Rest is not earned through productivity. It is a biological requirement and a psychological necessity — and for people whose inner conditions include a harsh inner critic or compulsive doing, it is an act of genuine self-advocacy.

The power of this framework is not in any single condition but in their combination. A day that includes all five, even in the most modest forms, is a day in which both inner and outer environments have been attended to. This consistency is the mechanism of change: not a single transformative insight, but the cumulative effect of daily tending.

The 5-a-Day of Wellbeing	Small daily actions
1. Noticing	5 min mindfulness practice; one mindful sensory moment; pause before responding
2. Moving	A walk; stretching; dancing; any movement that feels good
3. Connecting	One genuine conversation; a small act of kindness; five minutes of real contact
4. Creating	A journal sentence; a doodle; a photograph; a creative solution to a daily problem
5. Restoring	8 hours of sleep; 10 minutes of doing nothing; an activity with no required output

When the Conditions Take Root

For Rita, the question of creative practice was not abstract. She had been a dancer. She knew, in the precise physical way that dancers know things, exactly what it felt like to be fully inhabited by a moving body. She also knew what it felt like to stop. When the suggestion came that she might return to movement — not performance, not class, just movement at home, alone, without an audience or a standard — her first response was resistance. Her second, quieter response was recognition.

She now dances for ten minutes most mornings in her kitchen. She draws on the days she doesn't. She no longer needs it to be good. The tension and migraines have improved significantly. Mark, at his therapist's suggestion, joined a local football team with a friend and returned to the guitar for ten minutes each evening, meeting two conditions simultaneously. He no longer experiences panic attacks and his health anxiety has reduced. Brenda carved out one hour on Sunday mornings, non-negotiable, for pottery – something she had not done since university. None of these changes resolved everything. But each represented a daily signal to the self: my inner conditions matter. I am worth tending.

REFLECT

Which of the 5-a-Day of Wellbeing are already present in your life? Which are most depleted? Choose the one that feels most urgently needed and design one small, specific daily action that would begin to address it. Make it small enough that it is genuinely achievable tomorrow.

✎ *Take a moment to write your response in a notebook before continuing.*

No two orchids require exactly the same conditions. The research can tell you about light and moisture in general; it cannot tell you precisely what your orchid needs. Only you can discover that – through the noticing, the experimenting, the willingness to take your own inner experience seriously as data.

Tend the orchid. It will bloom.
The sensitivity was never the problem. It was always the advantage. Now you have the conditions to prove it.

What you do with that self-knowledge is the work of a lifetime. The science gives us frameworks, research findings, reliable mechanisms. The art is in the application: the irreplaceable process of discovering through patient experimentation and honest reflection which specific conditions, inner and outer, are yours.

Rita is still learning to protect her creative practice from her inner critic. Mark is slowly, painfully rebuilding his outer conditions after devastating loss and has returned to the guitar. Brenda is discovering, in her Sunday morning pottery, that she is a person as well as a function and that her own flourishing matters.

Their conditions are not yet optimal. Neither, probably, are yours. That is fine. Optimal is not a destination — it is a direction. The question is not whether you have arrived, but whether you are facing the right way and taking the next small step.

The orchid who finds their conditions doesn't only flourish for themselves. They become, quietly, better able to offer what they have to the people around them..

The tools and conditions explored in this book will serve most readers well, most of the time. But self-help has honest limits and recognising those limits is itself an act of self-knowledge, not defeat. The final chapter addresses something the conditions framework cannot always provide on its own: the particular kind of change that only becomes possible inside a skilled therapeutic relationship. If any part of you has been wondering whether what you are carrying might need more than a book can offer, the next few pages are written for you.

PART FOUR

Chapter 7: When to Seek Therapy and What It Offers

The tools and practices in this book are genuine and, consistently applied over time, they cultivate inner and outer conditions that support emotional wellbeing in ways that are measurable and lasting. But they are not sufficient for everyone, and not in all circumstances.

There are conditions in both the inner and outer environment that require more than self-help can provide. There are wounds that need a witness, not just a journal. There are belief systems so deeply established that they require a skilled therapeutic relationship to renegotiate. There are presentations such as serious depression, anxiety disorders, trauma, complex grief, and burnout where the right response is professional support, and where delay prolongs suffering unnecessarily.

Signs That More Support Is Needed

Indicators That Therapy May Be the Right Next Step

1. **Duration:** Persistent low mood, anxiety or emotional numbness lasting more than two to three weeks without clear cause, or disproportionate in intensity to a clear cause.

2. **Interference:** Psychological difficulties significantly interfering with your ability to work, maintain relationships or carry out daily activities.
3. **Safety:** Thoughts of harming yourself, not wanting to be alive, or feeling unable to keep yourself safe; however passive or vague these thoughts may seem.
4. **Withdrawal:** Progressive withdrawal from relationships, activities and environments that previously provided meaning and pleasure.
5. **Trauma**: A traumatic experience – past or recent – that continues to intrude through flashbacks, nightmares, hypervigilance or numbing more than one month after the event.
6. **Stuck:** You have applied the tools available to you with genuine commitment and your conditions continue to deteriorate rather than improve.

None of these signals permanent damage. They signal that the conditions you are navigating exceed what self-help is designed to address and that professional support could make an important difference.

What to Expect in Therapy

Many people who consider therapy for the first time do not know what to expect. The initial session is usually an assessment in both directions: the therapist understands your situation and you evaluate whether you feel sufficiently comfortable with this person to do difficult work. Expect questions about your history – relationships, work, symptoms, what brings you now. You do not need to have it all clear. Confusion and uncertainty are welcome.

Therapy is not a linear process. There are sessions that feel transformative and others that feel slow or puzzling. The therapeutic relationship — the working alliance between you and your therapist — is the most important mechanism of change, regardless of the approach used. If after four or five sessions you do not feel a basic sense of safety and of being understood, it is reasonable to raise this openly or to consider a different therapist. Fit matters.

What Therapy Can Offer

Therapy provides something no book can: a reliable, consistent, non-judgemental relationship with a person specifically trained to help you understand your inner conditions and cultivate more nourishing ones. The therapeutic relationship is not an incidental feature of therapy. Research consistently demonstrates it to be one of the primary mechanisms of change.

Cognitive Behavioural Therapy (CBT)

CBT works directly with thinking patterns and behavioural responses. It is structured, practical and collaborative, offering specific tools that can be applied between sessions and that outlast the therapeutic relationship itself. It is particularly effective for anxiety, depression, insomnia, OCD and phobias.

Compassion-Focused Therapy (CFT)

CFT addresses the quality of the inner relationship and the harshness of the inner critic. For people whose core beliefs centre on shame and self-criticism, it offers a specifically targeted and deeply transformative approach. It is particularly relevant for orchid-sensitive people with a strong self-critical pattern, and for people like Brenda whose suffering derives from decades of prioritising others' needs over their own.

Mindfulness-Based Cognitive Therapy (MBCT)

MBCT combines CBT tools with sustained mindfulness practice. It is especially well-evidenced for recurrent depression and for the kind of ruminative, self-amplifying thinking that keeps people stuck, the mental equivalent of a record that cannot find its groove.

Psychodynamic and Integrative Approaches

Psychodynamic approaches explore the deeper roots of inner conditions — the early relational experiences and formative beliefs that lie beneath the surface patterns. They are valuable when cognitive understanding seems insufficient: when someone can identify their patterns perfectly and yet cannot change them. The focus is less on techniques and more on the relationship itself as the agent of change.

Arts-Based Therapies

Art therapy, music therapy, dramatherapy and movement therapy bring the creative dimension into the therapeutic relationship itself. They are particularly valuable for people for whom verbal processing is insufficient: where the difficulty is primarily somatic, preverbal, or too raw to approach directly through language. For orchid-sensitive people with a strong connection to creative expression, arts-based therapy may feel like the most natural fit of all.

Finding the Right Fit

The relationship matters as much as the approach. When considering a therapist, pay attention to your felt sense with that person: do you feel safe? Heard? Genuinely met? The first session is always an evaluation in both directions. You are also assessing whether this person and approach are right for you. Asking a therapist about their training, experience and approach before the first session is entirely appropriate. Most professionals offer an initial consultation without commitment. Use that time to notice how you feel, not only what is said.

Seeking therapy is not a failure to cope. It is the recognition that some conditions require more than self-cultivation — and the wisdom to act on that recognition.

Some final thoughts

You began this book by locating yourself on a spectrum. Perhaps you recognised yourself immediately – in the sensitivity to atmosphere, the depth of processing, the nervous system that registers everything. Perhaps you arrived here depleted, in conditions that had been wrong for too long, wondering whether things could be different. They can. Not because you will become someone else, or because the world will become easier, but because you now have something you did not have before: a language for your experience, a map of your conditions, and a set of tools for tending them. The orchid does not become a dandelion overnight. It does not need to. It needs only the right light, the right care, the right conditions – and the patience to trust that when those conditions are right, it will bloom.

That patience, that tending, that quiet daily commitment to your own flourishing – that is not selfishness. It is the most important work you will ever do. And it begins, as all the best things do, simply: with noticing where you are, and taking one small step toward the conditions you need.

For further support, or to explore whether individual or group therapy is the right next step, please visit:

www.orquidiatherapy.com

If *The Orchid Mind* has resonated with you, or perhaps it gave you a language for something you've long felt but couldn't name, I would be genuinely grateful if you would leave a short review on Amazon. You don't need to write much. Even two sentences telling other readers what the book meant to you makes an enormous difference for an independent author.

Appendix: Quick Reference — Tools & Questionnaires

The following tools are referenced throughout this book. Return to them as needed — familiarity through repeated use is what builds the conditions of change.

Chapter 1 — The Orchid Hypothesis

- Sensitivity Spectrum Self-Assessment (Where Are You Right Now?)
- Visual Dandelion–Orchid Spectrum Scale

Chapter 4 — Cultivating Inner Conditions

- Comprehensive Thinking Errors Table with Rebalancing Questions
- The Thought Record (five-step CBT cognitive restructuring)
- The Worry Period Technique
- The Values Library (eight domains, 80+ values)
- Values Clarification Exercise (ACT) — six steps
- Five-Minute Foundational Mindfulness Practice
- The Self-Compassion Break (Neff)
- CBT for Insomnia (CBT-I) Technique Table

Chapter 5 — Cultivating Outer Conditions

- Optimal Work Conditions Questionnaire (15 items, five domains)
- Mapping Your Relational Conditions

Chapter 6 — Creative Rituals

- Five Principles for a Sustainable Creative Practice
- Menu of Creative Modalities with starter practices for each

Conclusion — Putting It Together

- The 5-a-Day of Wellbeing Framework (Noticing, Moving, Connecting, Creating, Restoring)

Progress Tracker

This book is designed to be worked, not only read. Use the table below to record which tools you have tried, when you first used them, and what you noticed. Returning to earlier entries over time is itself a mindfulness practice — it shows you how far you have come.

Tool / Practice	Date first used	Repeated (X)	What I noticed
Orchid/Dandelion Self-Assessment			
Thought Record (CBT)			
The Worry Period Technique			
Values Clarification Exercise			
Five-Minute Mindfulness Practice			
The Self-Compassion Break			
Work Conditions Questionnaire			
Relational Conditions Mapping			
My Chosen Creative Practice			
The 5-a-Day of Wellbeing			

Glossary of Key Terms

The following terms are used throughout this book. This brief reference is intended for readers who may find psychological language unfamiliar — not as exhaustive definitions, but as points of entry.

Amygdala

A brain structure that acts as the organism's threat-detection system. In orchid-sensitive people, or those under chronic stress, the amygdala may maintain a state of elevated vigilance, responding to social and psychological threats as though they were physical ones.

Neuroplasticity

The brain's capacity to reorganise itself by forming new neural connections throughout life. Repeated practice — including creative practice, mindfulness and cognitive restructuring — literally reshapes the brain over time.

Cortisol

The primary stress hormone, released by the adrenal glands in response to perceived threat. Chronic cortisol impairs mood, memory, the immune system and sleep.

Vagus Nerve

The longest nerve of the autonomic nervous system, connecting the brain to the heart, lungs and gut. Vagal stimulation — through deep breathing, singing, social contact and gentle movement — activates the parasympathetic state of rest and restoration.

CBT — Cognitive Behavioural Therapy

A well-established, evidence-based psychotherapy approach focusing on the relationship between thoughts, feelings and behaviours. It teaches specific skills for identifying and modifying unhelpful thinking patterns.

CBT-I — CBT for Insomnia

An adaptation of CBT specifically for chronic sleep difficulties. Includes sleep restriction, stimulus control, sleep hygiene and cognitive restructuring of beliefs about sleep.

CFT — Compassion-Focused Therapy

Developed by Paul Gilbert, CFT integrates evolutionary neuroscience with mindfulness and compassion practices to address shame and self-criticism. Particularly relevant for those with a harsh inner critic.

ACT — Acceptance and Commitment Therapy

A third-wave CBT approach focusing on values clarification, acceptance of difficult thoughts without struggling against them, and commitment to values-aligned action.

The Three Emotional Systems

Paul Gilbert's model of emotional regulation: the *Threat System* (detects danger, activates fight-or-flight); the *Drive System* (motivates goal pursuit); the *Soothing System* (promotes contentment, safety and connection). Optimal wellbeing requires access to all three. Creative activity is one of the most reliable routes into the *Soothing System.*

The Orchid Hypothesis

The theory proposed by W. Thomas Boyce and Bruce Ellis that human beings differ in environmental sensitivity on a spectrum from dandelion (robust, adaptive) to orchid (highly sensitive, highly responsive). Originally developed through research in developmental paediatrics and evolutionary psychology, the hypothesis proposes that the same underlying responsiveness that creates vulnerability in adverse conditions also creates heightened capacity for flourishing in nurturing ones. This responsiveness may have genetic roots for some people, but is also shaped by experience, relational history, and the cumulative demands placed on a person's system over time. The orchid's apparent fragility and its extraordinary bloom are two expressions of the same quality — and that quality can shift across a lifetime.

The Highly Sensitive Person (HSP) Framework

A concept developed by psychologist Elaine Aron, who first identified and named high sensitivity as a distinct trait in 1991. Aron's research described approximately 15–20% of the population as Highly Sensitive Persons — individuals with a more finely tuned nervous system that processes sensory and emotional information more deeply than most. HSPs tend to be easily overwhelmed by intense stimulation, deeply affected by others' moods and emotions, moved by art and music, and in need of more downtime to recover from busy environments. Aron's framework emphasises that high sensitivity is a neutral trait — neither a disorder nor a superpower — whose expression depends substantially on the conditions in which a person lives and develops. The HSP concept remains an active area of scientific refinement: some researchers prefer to describe sensitivity as a continuously distributed trait rather than a distinct personality type, and the relationship between Aron's HSP model and Boyce and Belsky's differential susceptibility research continues to be explored.

Differential Susceptibility

A theoretical framework developed by developmental psychologist Jay Belsky, building on the Orchid Hypothesis. Where earlier diathesis-stress models emphasised that sensitive individuals are more vulnerable to adversity, Belsky's differential susceptibility hypothesis proposes that sensitivity operates symmetrically: sensitive individuals are more affected by their environments in both directions, more harmed by poor conditions, but also more enhanced by good ones. In Belsky's formulation, sensitivity is not a vulnerability but a heightened responsiveness to context. Sensitive children placed in high-quality environments — warm parenting, supportive schools, rich relationships — often outperform their less sensitive peers, not just match them. This reframing is central to the argument of this book: the trait that feels like a liability in the wrong conditions is the same trait that becomes the advantage in the right ones.

Flow
A psychological state of complete, effortless engagement in an activity, described by Csikszentmihalyi. Flow is associated with pleasure, loss of self-consciousness and high performance, and is one of the states most directly accessible through creative practice.

Gut Microbiome
The community of trillions of microorganisms living in the digestive tract. Research by John Cryan, Ted Dinan and others has established a significant bidirectional connection between gut microbiome health and mental health — influencing mood, stress reactivity and cognition via the vagus nerve. Approximately 90% of the body's serotonin is produced in the gut, making diet a direct factor in psychological inner conditions.

Bibliography

The following works have informed this book directly. Readers wishing to explore any dimension in greater depth will find these an invaluable starting point.

The Orchid/Dandelion Hypothesis & Developmental Psychology

Aron, E. N. (1996). The Highly Sensitive Person: How to Thrive When the World Overwhelms You. Broadway Books.

Boyce, W. T. (2019). The Orchid and the Dandelion: Why Some Children Struggle and How All Can Thrive. Bluebird.

Ellis, B. J., & Boyce, W. T. (2008). Biological sensitivity to context. Current Directions in Psychological Science, 17(3), 183–187. https://doi.org/10.1111/j.1467-8721.2008.00571.x

Belsky, J., & Pluess, M. (2009). Beyond diathesis stress: Differential susceptibility to environmental influences. Psychological Bulletin, 135(6), 885–908 . https://doi.org/10.1037/a0017376

Pluess, M. (2015). Individual differences in environmental sensitivity. Child Development Perspectives, 9(3), 138–143.

Pluess, M., & Belsky, J. (2013). Vantage sensitivity: Individual differences in response to positive experiences. *Psychological Bulletin, 139*(4), 901–916. https://doi.org/10.1037/a0030196

Albert, D., Belsky, D. W., Crowley, D. M., Latendresse, S. J., Aliev, F., Riley, B., Vladimirov, V., Dick, D. M., & Dodge, K. A. (2015). Can genetics predict response to complex behavioral interventions? Evidence from a genetic analysis of the Fast Track Randomized Control Trial. Journal of Policy Analysis and Management, 34(3), 497–518.

Plomin, R., & Daniels, D. (1987). Why are children in the same family so different from one another? Behavioral and Brain Sciences, 10(1), 1–16 . https://doi.org/10.1017/S0140525X00056272

Cognitive Behavioural Therapy

Beck, A. T. (1979). Cognitive Therapy of Depression. Guilford Press.

Beck, J. S. (2011). Cognitive Behavior Therapy: Basics and Beyond (2nd ed.). Guilford Press.

Burns, D. D. (1980). Feeling Good: The New Mood Therapy. William Morrow.

Clark, D. A., & Beck, A. T. (2010). Cognitive Therapy of Anxiety Disorders: Science and Practice. Guilford Press.

Leahy, R. L. (2017). Cognitive Therapy Techniques: A Practitioner's Guide (2nd ed.). Guilford Press.

Greenberger, D., & Padesky, C. A. (2015). Mind Over Mood: Change How You Feel by Changing the Way You Think (2nd ed.). Guilford Press.

CBT for Insomnia

Espie, C. A. (2006). Overcoming Insomnia and Sleep Problems: A Self-Help Guide Using Cognitive Behavioral Techniques. Robinson.

Harvey, A. G. (2002). A cognitive model of insomnia. Behaviour Research and Therapy, 40(8), 869–893 https://doi.org/10.1016/S0005-7967(01)00061-4

Morin, C. M., & Espie, C. A. (2003). Insomnia: A Clinical Guide to Assessment and Treatment. Springer.

Riemann, D., & Perlis, M. L. (2009). The treatments of chronic insomnia: A review of benzodiazepine receptor agonists and psychological and behavioral therapies. Sleep Medicine Reviews, 13(3), 205–214.

Mindfulness and Compassion-Focused Therapy

Kabat-Zinn, J. (1990). Full Catastrophe Living: Using the Wisdom of Your Body and Mind to Face Stress, Pain and Illness. Delacorte Press.

Williams, M., Teasdale, J., Segal, Z., & Kabat-Zinn, J. (2007). The Mindful Way Through Depression. Guilford Press.

Gilbert, P. (2010). The Compassionate Mind: A New Approach to Life's Challenges. Constable.

Gilbert, P. (2009). Compassion-Focused Therapy. Routledge.

Neff, K. (2011). Self-Compassion: Stop Beating Yourself Up and Leave Insecurity Behind. William Morrow.

Neff, K. D., & Germer, C. K. (2013). A pilot study and randomized controlled trial of the mindful self-compassion program. Journal of Clinical Psychology, 69(1), 28–44 https://doi.org/10.1002/jclp.21923

Acceptance and Commitment Therapy & Values

Hayes, S. C., Strosahl, K. D., & Wilson, K. G. (2011). Acceptance and Commitment Therapy: The Process and Practice of Mindful Change (2nd ed.). Guilford Press.

Harris, R. (2008). The Happiness Trap: How to Stop Struggling and Start Living. Exisle Publishing.

Harris, R. (2009). ACT Made Simple: An Easy-to-Read Primer on Acceptance and Commitment Therapy. New Harbinger.

Dolan, P. (2014). Happiness by Design: Finding Pleasure and Purpose in Everyday Life. Allen Lane.

Neuroscience and Trauma

Van der Kolk, B. (2014). The Body Keeps the Score: Brain, Mind and Body in the Healing of Trauma. Viking.

Siegel, D. J. (2010). Mindsight: The New Science of Personal Transformation. Bantam Books.

LeDoux, J. (1996). The Emotional Brain: The Mysterious Underpinnings of Emotional Life. Simon & Schuster.

Porges, S. W. (2011). The Polyvagal Theory: Neurophysiological Foundations of Emotions, Attachment, Communication, and Self-regulation. W. W. Norton & Company.

Merzenich, M. M. (2013). Soft-Wired: How the New Science of Brain Plasticity Can Change Your Life. Parnassus Publishing.

Malchiodi, C. A. (2011). Handbook of Art Therapy (2nd ed.). Guilford Press.

Malchiodi, C. A. (2020). Trauma and Expressive Arts Therapy: Brain, Body, and Imagination in the Healing Process. Guilford Press.

Creativity and Wellbeing

Csikszentmihalyi, M. (1990). Flow: The Psychology of Optimal Experience. Harper & Row.

May, R. (1975). The Courage to Create. W. W. Norton & Company.

Pennebaker, J. W. (1997). Opening Up: The Healing Power of Expressing Emotions. Guilford Press.

Pennebaker, J. W., & Smyth, J. M. (2016). Opening Up by Writing It Down: How Expressive Writing Improves Health and Eases Emotional Pain (3rd ed.). Guilford Press.

Stuckey, H. L., & Nobel, J. (2010). The connection between art, healing, and public health: A review of current literature. American Journal of Public Health, 100(2), 254–263. https://doi.org/10.2105/AJPH.2008.156497

Lewis, C., & Lovatt, P. J. (2013). Breaking away from set patterns of thinking: Improvisation and divergent thinking. Thinking Skills and Creativity, 9, 46–58 https://doi.org/10.1016/j.tsc.2013.03.001

Richards, R. (Ed.). (2007). Everyday Creativity and New Views of Human Nature. American Psychological Association.

Kaimal, G., Ray, K., & Muniz, J. (2016). Reduction of cortisol levels and participants' responses following art making. Art Therapy: Journal of the American Art Therapy Association, 33(2), 74–80. https://doi.org/10.1080/07421656.2016.1166832

Fancourt, D., & Finn, S. (2019). What is the evidence on the role of the arts in improving health and wellbeing? A scoping review. WHO Regional Office for Europe https://www.euro.who.int/en/publications/abstracts/what-is-the-evidence-on-the-role-of-the-arts-in-improving-health-and-wellbeing-a-scoping-review-2019

Brown, S., & Vaughan, C. (2009). Play: How It Shapes the Brain, Opens the Imagination, and Invigorates the Soul. Avery.

Koelsch, S. (2012). Brain and Music. Wiley-Blackwell.

Koelsch, S. (2014). Brain correlates of music-evoked emotions. Nature Reviews Neuroscience, 15(3), 170–180 https://doi.org/10.1038/nrn3666

Fancourt, D., Aufegger, L., & Williamon, A. (2015). Low-stress and high-stress singing have contrasting effects on glucocorticoid response. Frontiers in Psychology, 6, Article 1242. https://doi.org/10.3389/fpsyg.2015.01242

Lovatt, P. (2020). The Dance Cure: The Surprising Secret to Being Smarter, Stronger, Happier. Short Books.

National Centre for Creative Health & All-Party Parliamentary Group on Arts, Health and Wellbeing. (2023). Creative health review: How policy can embrace creative health. NCCH. https://ncch.org.uk/creative-health-review

Jensen, A., Holt, N., Honda, S., & Bungay, H. (2024). The impact of arts on prescription on individual health and wellbeing: A systematic review with meta-analysis. Frontiers in Public Health, 12, Article 1412306. https://doi.org/10.3389/fpubh.2024.1412306

Fancourt, D., & Steptoe, A. (2019). The art of life and death: 14 year follow-up analyses of associations between arts engagement and mortality in the English Longitudinal Study of Ageing. BMJ, 367, Article l6377. https://doi.org/10.1136/bmj.l6377

Nutrition, Sleep and Physical Wellbeing

Korn, L. (2016). Nutrition Essentials for Mental Health: A Complete Guide to the Food-Mood Connection. W. W. Norton & Company.

Yano, J. M., Yu, K., Donaldson, G. P., Shastri, G. G., Ann, P., Ma, L., Nagler, C. R., Ismagilov, R. F., Mazmanian, S. K., & Hsiao, E. Y. (2015). Indigenous bacteria from the gut microbiota regulate host serotonin biosynthesis. Cell, 161(2), 264–276.

Cryan, J. F., & Dinan, T. G. (2012). Mind-altering microorganisms: The impact of the gut microbiota on brain and behaviour. Nature Reviews Neuroscience, 13(10), 701–712. https://doi.org/10.1038/nrn3346

Cryan, J. F., & Dinan, T. G. (2017). The Psychobiotic Revolution: Mood, Food, and the New Science of the Gut-Brain Connection. National Geographic.

Campbell-McBride, N. (2010). Gut and Psychology Syndrome. Medinform Publishing.

Holford, P. (2007). Optimum Nutrition for the Mind. Piatkus.

McEwen, B. S. (2002). Estrogen actions throughout the brain. Recent Progress in Hormone Research, 57, 357–384. https://doi.org/10.1210/rp.57.1.357

Lokuge, S., Frey, B. N., Foster, J. A., Soares, C. N., & Steiner, M. (2011). Depression in women: Windows of vulnerability and new insights into the link between estrogen and serotonin. Journal of Clinical Psychiatry, 72(11), e1563–e1569 . https://doi.org/10.4088/JCP.11com07089

Soares, C. N., & Frey, B. N. (2010). Challenges and opportunities to manage depression during the menopausal transition and beyond. Psychiatric Clinics of North America, 33(2), 295–308. https://doi.org/10.1016/j.psc.2010.01.007

Blakemore, S. J., Burnett, S., & Dahl, R. E. (2010). The role of puberty in the developing adolescent brain. Human Brain Mapping, 31(6), 926–933. https://doi.org/10.1002/hbm.21052

Newson, L. (2021). Preparing for the Perimenopause and Menopause. Penguin.

University of Exeter. (2015). Green exercise: Nature's healing power. Retrieved from http://www.exeter.ac.uk/research/impact/nature-healing-power

Brooks, S., & Pritchard, S. (2020). The role of exercise in recovery from mental illness: A systematic review and meta-analysis. JAMA Psychiatry, 77(7), 711-719 doi:10.1001/jamapsychiatry.2020.0358

Social Connection, Loneliness and Community

Cacioppo, J. T., & Patrick, W. (2008). Loneliness: Human Nature and the Need for Social Connection. W. W. Norton & Company.

New Economics Foundation. (2008). Five Ways to Wellbeing: The Evidence. NEF.

Holt-Lunstad, J., Smith, T. B., & Layton, J. B. (2010). Social relationships and mortality risk: A meta-analytic review. PLOS Medicine, 7(7), e1000316.

Rogers, C. R. (1957). The necessary and sufficient conditions of therapeutic personality change. Journal of Consulting Psychology, 21(2), 95–103. https://doi.org/10.1037/h0045357

Rogers, C. R. (1961). On Becoming a Person: A Therapist's View of Psychotherapy. Houghton Mifflin.

Gratitude and Positive Psychology

Emmons, R. A., & McCullough, M. E. (2003). Counting blessings versus burdens: An experimental investigation of gratitude and subjective wellbeing in daily life. Journal of Personality and Social Psychology, 84(2), 377–389 . https://doi.org/10.1037/0022-3514.84.2.377

Emmons, R. A. (2007). Thanks! How the New Science of Gratitude Can Make You Happier. Houghton Mifflin.

Seligman, M. E. P., Steen, T. A., Park, N., & Peterson, C. (2005). Positive psychology progress: Empirical validation of interventions. American Psychologist, 60(5), 410–421. https://doi.org/10.1037/0003-066X.60.5.410

Wood, A. M., Froh, J. J., & Geraghty, A. W. A. (2010). Gratitude and wellbeing: A review and theoretical integration. Clinical Psychology Review, 30(7), 890–905 https://doi.org/10.1016/j.cpr.2010.03.005

Seligman, M. E. P. (2011). Flourish: A Visionary New Understanding of Happiness and Wellbeing. Free Press.

Watkins, P. C. (2014). Gratitude and the Good Life: Toward a Psychology of Appreciation. Springer.

Depression and Burnout

Cantopher, T. (2012). Depressive Illness: The Curse of the Strong (3rd ed.). Sheldon Press.

Moore, T. (1992). Care of the Soul: A Guide for Cultivating Depth and Sacredness in Everyday Life. HarperCollins.

Maslach, C., & Leiter, M. P. (2016). Burnout. In G. Fink (Ed.), Stress: Concepts, Cognition, Emotion, and Behavior. Academic Press.

Professional and Practice Background

Foerschner, A. (2010). The history of mental illness: From skull drills to happy pills. Inquiries Journal, 2(9).

Hull, A., & Morphew-Lu, E. (2016). Introduction to Nutritional Psychology. JFK University Nutritional Psychology Certificate Programme.

Zecevic-Gonzalez, S. (2015). My creative practice. Private Practice, Spring 2015. British Association for Counselling and Psychotherapy.

About the Author

Sandra Zecevic-Gonzalez is a Counselling Psychologist and Accredited Cognitive Behavioural Therapist practising in West London. She is the founder of Orquidia Therapy, where she works with individuals navigating anxiety, depression, burnout and life transitions, with a specialist interest in the intersection of creativity and psychological wellbeing.

The Orchid Mind sets out the integrative framework she has developed across twenty years of private practice – bringing together the Orchid Hypothesis, CBT, compassion-focused work and the science of creativity into a coherent clinical approach that she uses with clients navigating sensitivity, burnout and the slow work of finding their conditions. She has written articles for the British Association for Counselling and Psychotherapy on the role of creative practice in therapeutic work and nutritional psychology. She has published in Families Magazine UK and numerous articles and blog posts for websites of counselling and psychology services in London.

The Orchid Mind is her first book.

www.orquidiatherapy.com

If *The Orchid Mind* has resonated with you, or perhaps it gave you a language for something you've long felt but couldn't name, I would be genuinely grateful if you would leave a short review on Amazon. You don't need to write much. Even two sentences telling other readers what the book meant to you makes an enormous difference for an independent author.

Thank you.

www.ingramcontent.com/pod-product-compliance
Lightning Source LLC
LaVergne TN
LVHW010111170826
845678LV00012B/2345

9781067612139